THE ORIGINAL SANCTUARY

By Marc Owings and David Terry

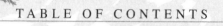

TABLE OF CONTENTS

CHAPTER 1
Tales from the Ditch

He was born in one world, I in another. Our pasts paint the picture of two men growing up in two opposite ditches of the same road. Different worlds. Different wounds. Different devastations. Had we met as teenagers, we wouldn't have even been friends. In school, he walked on one side of the hall and I walked on the other. There was a clear separation of our worlds. However, we met in a mid-life collision that continues to radically alter our hearts today.

Now we travel side by side, walking down the highway of life . . . in the abundant life God intended us to have. We were two brothers from the same Father, and we found each other. This is our story.

 DAVID

I was Baptist before I was Christian. Sundays, Wednesdays, visitation, prayer meetings, you name it . . . if the church doors were open, my family was there. At the age of 7, I gave my heart to Christ. I got down on my leopard-print bedspread and gave all that a 7 year old can muster. I vividly remember my mom and dad telling me, "David, it's all about the heart." They were more right than I knew at the time. It was all about my heart. But somewhere along the way, I strayed from their wisdom.

From the cradle in the church nursery to the pulpit where I sang and preached as a young man in the ministry, church was my comfort zone. The do's and don'ts, the praises and condemnations, the expectations and taboos molded my whole world, and I learned to live within the boundaries. I was good at it. I was good at being good. According to the rulebook, as far as anyone else could tell, I was a model Christian.

Now, there is nothing wrong with the world I grew up in. The core teachings of this book are based on and laced with the foundations that I received as a young man growing up in the church. Scripture was taught. Spiritual disciplines were encouraged. My mother and father surrounded me and my brother with some really good stuff. The problem was, though I was outwardly compliant, I was inwardly rebellious.

I would do the right thing, say the right thing and even believe the right thing, all the while, becoming more and more calloused and hard to the innermost longings of my heart. Over time, my heart began to disengage and my mind took the lead. Instead of using the tools of the Word to draw closer to the heart of God, I allowed them to become an end in themselves. When the quest for knowledge really set in, I unknowingly traded my heart for intellectualism and a doable list of rules and responses. I had no balance. I didn't know how to exist with an engaged mind and a tender spirit. And it almost killed me.

Deep down, I could not deny my heart. No matter how good I made myself look, I struggled with gross sin on the inside. Doing all the right things was not making me a good person; it wasn't even making me happy. The only way I could keep up the façade of being "a good guy" was to suppress what I knew to be true. I was a poser. I was a fake.

Disconnecting emotionally, I focused all my energy on accomplishing the non-tangible things in my world – I read my Bible, went to church, paid my tithe, taught, spoke, led worship, didn't drink, smoke or cheat on my taxes – but I spent very little energy on anything authentic or sincere. That was life for me . . . a life that turned out to be death.

By my late 20's, I was a mess (though no one knew it). My life had become a blur of inconsistencies. I was one thing on the outside and another on the inside. I was conflicted, confused, torn and in the ditch. I had divided my family, business, ministry, financial and personal life into what I thought were "manageable compartments." I became an expert at never allowing them to mix. The relationships in one area were never introduced to anyone in another. If they had mixed, my cover would have been blown.

In business with a brilliant, non-believer I became completely confused and lost. My compass no longer pointed North. My business "compartment" exploded and sent shrapnel through every other area of my life. A visit from the State of Texas Attorney General's office and an appearance on the witness stand in a federal courtroom were the low-lights of this season of my life. I was completely broken in every way.

Thousand of thoughts and feelings a day raced through my mind. But I still never let them out. For me to let them out would seem to be "imperfect." My outer image had to be polished and controlled. All the while I was depressed, oppressed and fearful. I was hopelessly afraid of not being successful, of not making it. I was afraid to try, but too afraid not to.

Unable to communicate on a true heart level with my wife, our marriage was on the brink of implosion after just a few years. I was carrying around a ton of junk, but didn't know how to cope with any of it. Since my depression, perfectionism and fear were life-long roots in me, I thought that I was "normal" (whatever that is). In reality, those things in me with which I was most comfortable were the very things that were killing me.

*For me to deal with my twisted thinking and my deadened heart
would require me to expose my alter identity for the lie that it was.
My wife knew my issues better than anyone because she lived with
me day in and day out. It was overwhelmingly frustrating to her to
know the real me and yet have to deal with the poser I insisted on
hiding behind.*

*Out of the brokenness God begin to resurrect my heart. Slowly
but surely I was coming back. Back to whom I was intended to be.
In the Spring of 2002, on the side of a mountain in New Mexico,
God yanked me into a life that I couldn't have ever imagined. I
didn't have to pose anymore. He showed me that no matter how I
presented myself to the world, the truth was that the only person I
was really fooling was me. My Father grabbed me by the back of
the neck and forced me to look at what I had become. When I saw
what He saw, it broke me.*

*Where I had been was never in His heart, but He let me go anyway.
He came after me and redeemed my life out of that ditch. Now, I
can't go back. I won't go back. I will never be the same again.
I have been rescued by the hand of God.*

David

 MARC

*I grew up in a middle class family of five, and for the most part, my
childhood reflected a bizarre combination of Huckleberry Finn and
the song "Born to be Wild."*

*My dad was an intellectual genius. Despite his high IQ, he
didn't have the skill set or patience to father my older brother
and younger sister, much less a free spirit like me. Though he was
a smart guy, his moral compass was a bit off . . . designing and
building strip joints and nightclubs was where he scratched out*

his living. At a very early age I understood that intelligence does not equal success or knowing what the right thing to do is. Smart people do stupid things!

My mom was and is a saint to me. She was extremely loving, stable and funny. Though she tried to keep all the madness in check, she was unable to save me from the tidal wave that was coming at me with full and destructive intent.

By the time I was twelve years old, I was sexually active and began to experiment with smoking pot with the older kids in the neighborhood. Soon, I began to abuse drugs and alcohol. In high school, I was fun and crazy, the guy who planned the keg parties instead of just attending them. I was a fighter and ready to prove it for less than the drop of a hat. Life was a party, and I lived it up.

I had four goals back then that I achieved with great success: get high, get drunk, get the girl and get in a fight. I didn't care if I won the fight or lost the girl. I just wanted to feel something, even if it meant someone beating me unconscious, which seemed to become a ritual with me. Too many weekends to count, my family found me beaten beyond recognition or blacked out just short of our front door. To be honest, I thought that living to the ripe old age of 21 was impossible.

With no conscience, unbridled appetites and uncontrollable desires I was driven to pursue all that the world had to offer. "God" was just a concept to me. It was a vague idea I had heard of but was never really interested in. As a child, I never once heard the gospel message. So when my cousin Jeff opened the Bible and read it to me when I was 19-years-old, it was all new.

Like my father, I was a reader, familiar with both modern and classic literature. But after hearing just a few words from the Bible, I knew it was different from anything I had ever encountered. When I began reading it for myself, it was like seeing a new color for the first time. It was alive!

In the middle of the book of Isaiah (one of the most unlikely places for a novice like myself to be reading), I saw God for who He was. The words ministered to me, and I just got it. Jesus is the Son of God, and through Him I could find a place at the King's table. Until that moment, my life had no aim except to bring me pleasure and escape my lonely reality. But when I received God's Word and faith in Jesus, I was free to be who God called me to be. Yes, I was born to be wild and I knew there was a mystery and fight ahead of me that would be unlike anything I had ever experienced before.

I'm not saying everything in my life straightened up overnight. I remained involved in things I shouldn't have for a while. But there was something different inside of me. Life took on new meaning and purpose. I had met God, and He was changing me. After years of searching for a painkiller and coming up empty, I finally found forgiveness through a real, authentic relationship with God. The loneliness was gone.

Marc

Our stories are not noteworthy because we have accomplished anything great. Anything good in our lives has been deposited there straight from the throne of our good and merciful God. God reached down into both of our ditches and pulled us out. The cure for our terminal diseases, as different as they were, was the same – grace from a loving God who has the power to make all things new.

We met at the cross and realized that we have the same Father in heaven. We both were called to be about the family business. Today, we are looking for those who are struggling to get out of their ditches of despair and receive their God-given purpose and destiny. We are looking for our brothers and sisters.

If you are looking for a book that will fill your brain with more information, burn this one, give it to your brother-in-law for Christmas or use it as a doorstop. Whatever you do though, don't read it.

But if you are longing for an honest look inside your heart, keep reading. This book is about taking all that the world has placed on you and religion has stolen from you and redeeming it as fuel for the life that God has created for you to live. It is a journey into the meaning and significance of life. It is a treasure map that will lead you to the original sanctuary . . . your heart.

Would you like to hear the rest of the story?

CHAPTER 2
The Tree House

"I WENT TO THE WOODS BECAUSE I WISHED
TO LIVE DELIBERATELY . . . AND NOT, WHEN
I CAME TO DIE, DISCOVER THAT I HAD
NOT LIVED." HENRY DAVID THOREAU

MARC

Even though I grew up in the city of Fort Worth, Texas, I've always considered myself a country boy. The great outdoors captivates me – the sights and smells, the landscape and creatures, the mystery and adventure. As boys, my brother and I would spend every spare minute venturing into the woods around our home. After school and especially during the summers, we would jump fences, climb trees and fish for crawdads until dark settled and drove us back to civilization.

Nothing could keep our wild hearts from embarking on journeys, explorations and escapades into uncharted territories. One place we loved to go was guarded by a sign that read: "No Trespassing. Survivors Will Be Shot." Ha! That warning couldn't keep us away. If anything, it made what lay beyond even more appealing.

My brother and I, along with our neighborhood buddies, were always either building something up or tearing it down. One of my favorite memories is when we all worked together to build a tree house. Now, this wasn't just any tree house. It was THE tree house. We took the endeavor very seriously. It wasn't a one day, throw-something-together-and-forget-about-it-later kind of deal. This project was an all out assault on a giant oak tree that stood tall in an empty field behind our neighborhood.

Every Saturday and Sunday for weeks, a massive convoy of local boys descended on this construction site to advance the cause of human architecture and creativity. Armed with borrowed, stolen and broken tools, we attacked that tree, determined to turn it into the greatest tree house in the world. We hauled load after load of wood from a nearby construction site. Still too young to drive, we didn't use Ford or Chevy trucks, but red wagons and our fathers' wheel barrows. Over those weeks we must have stolen enough wood to have built our own juvenile detention center. With every rusty nail and crooked saw, we built to our hearts' content. "Hand me another two-by-four!" my brother shouted.

"How long?" I asked.

"I don't care. Just gimme one. It'll fit."

There were no blue prints to follow. None of us had actually mapped out a plan. We didn't need one. The only absolute was that we were building a tree house. It didn't matter to us what it was supposed to look like or how long it should take us. We just started in the middle and worked our way out. It was a boys' paradise. No teacher to grade our work. No parents to tell us it was far too dangerous. We were on our own, building and creating, and we loved it!

Looking back, I'm sure the sight of us was hilarious: throwing lumber into this massive oak tree, hammering wood strips, uncut and unmeasured, in any place that seemed right. In the end, though, it was obvious that this one-of-a-kind masterpiece was designed in the hearts of childhood kings. For those of us who put in the sweat and poured in the heart, it was a priceless work of art.

With the completion of our tree-top kingdom, we all moved on to bigger and better things. There were other fences to jump and other properties to trespass on. However, for me and my brother, that tree house always remained special. It became our personal, private haven: the place where we hid when we were scared and the place we longed for when our hearts were hurt. When nothing in our world made sense, we went to the tree house. It was safe there. There was no pain, no rejection. In the tree house, there *was just me and my brother, alone with our thoughts, sorting out life. High above the world and its troubles, the tree house became our refuge, our asylum, our safe house . . . our sanctuary.*

Marc

THE ORIGINAL SANCTUARY

As children, without inhibitions or fears to hold us back, we were free to become exactly who God made us to be. Building that tree house is how the Creator intended us to live . . . and still intends for us to live today. The Bible never calls us "adults of God." It says we are "children of God" (John 1:12 NIV), and that means we were created to live in the daily dawning of wide-eyed wonder at our adventure. Our destiny is to live out the life-long relationship of a carefree child with his loving Father.

Building and creating are a sacred part of God's heart. In the beginning, He too embarked upon a massive "building adventure." Of course, when He created, He did so on a much grander scale. His "tree house" was beyond compare.

God did not have to rummage through scraps or steal from the local contractor to get His material. He started with *nothing* and created everything. In fact, He didn't even use His hands to piece it all together. The Bible says He spoke it into existence. There were no models or prototypes to test and ensure accuracy; He simply said "Let there be . . . " and every cell, biological system, color, structure and fragrance came into existence . . . every part of it just was.

But while the physical creation of God is astounding and breath-taking, the most amazing of His creations to us is the human heart – not the mechanical, blood-pumping organ in the left center of the chest, but the unseen heart that sits at the core of every human's being. Naked to the human eye, your heart is more marvelous than any of God's creation. Home to your desires and dreams, life to your spirit and conscience, your heart is unlike anything else God has made.

Think about your own heart. It's the place you store your private thoughts and protect your past. It's that place you labor to keep secret yet strangely long for someone else to know. It contains the DNA of who you are intended to be and is as unique as your fingerprints. Your heart is what makes you, you.

When God created the heart, He made it to mirror Him. When that group of boys built that tree house, they displayed the creative and inventive part of God's character. In the same way, God has placed a fingerprint of who He is on the hearts of each of His children. And He did that so our hearts could connect with His, commune with His.

Yes, the heart was intended to be a place of co-habitation. It is a place for two, a place of intimacy. When you go there, you can connect with God. That is what He intended when He placed your heart within you . . . He is waiting to meet with you.

 DAVID

In the summer of 1984, I took some college courses in Western Europe. During those nine weeks, I toured some of the most beautiful, unique cathedrals and churches in the world: Westminster Cathedral, Winchester Cathedral and St. Paul's Cathedral to name a few. Some of these buildings took thirty, forty and even fifty years to construct. The classic Gothic architecture, tediously hand-carved stone, crystal chandeliers and exquisite stained-glass windows were designed to enhance the construction of these "houses of God." However, in all of their

glory and beauty, these marvelous houses of worship are really only that . . . houses.

David

Churches and cathedrals are just buildings where people gather in hopes of encountering God. Even the most spectacular cathedral will pale in comparison to God's creation of His own home in the hearts of man. Before there was ever a physical tabernacle or temple, cathedral or church, God had designed a perfect place to commune with His beloved creation. Our hearts are His original sanctuary.

Webster dictionaries define *sanctuary* as a *"sacred place," "a place of giving refuge or asylum," "a private place"* and *"free of intrusion."*[1]

We have chosen this word carefully. There is a beautiful and magical mystery about such a place. Where is this place? How do I get there from here? It's in you! Your heart was created to be sacred – a place of refuge, privacy and asylum, free from the fear of intrusion.

God didn't just create this dwelling place in Billy Graham's or Mother Theresa's heart. This is not some secret club reserved for the "special people." He placed it in every single one of us. Stunning, isn't it? It's in you!

We may have fooled you into thinking that because we are writing a book we are good men worthy of such intimacy with God. We're not more worthy. Wrong! We know better. We get regular whiffs of our inner cesspools. We have a news flash for you. We're worse than you think! Our hearts are far from holy and perfect. Sometimes we wonder why God would ever choose to set up camp there. But He did. And He still does. His presence is what makes the difference.

It is a great joy and privilege to climb high into the sanctuary of the heart, far above the issues of this world, to the secret haven of worship. There, the Father whispers His love and truth and we are changed. You might be thinking this sanctuary we are speaking of is a figment of our imagination. But it's not. It's as real as the air we breathe. And it can be for you too.

ORIGINAL WORTH

Picasso Works Stolen From Granddaughter
By: Jean-Pierre Verges, Associated Press Writer
Wednesday-February 28, 2007
USA Today

Paris, France – At least two Picasso paintings, worth a total of nearly $66 million, were stolen from the house of the artist's granddaughter's house in Paris, police said Wednesday.

The paintings, "Maya and the Doll" and "Portrait of Jacqueline," disappeared overnight Monday to Tuesday from the chic 7th district, a Paris police official said.

The official said they were worth nearly $66 million. The director of the Picasso Museum, Anne Baldassari, said several paintings and drawings were stolen from the home of Diana Widmaier-Picasso . . .

Together, these two paintings were worth nearly $66 million. In the world that we live in, that is a ton of money! How could canvas, oil and color be that valuable to anyone?

The answer: First, they were created by a remarkably gifted artist. Because the paintings are his creation, they carry his name. Just the name Picasso invokes respect and authority in the world of art and culture. Pablo Picasso created these paintings with his own two hands. His signature gives them value. Second, they are original works. Original works of art by famous, renowned artists are intrinsically valuable. Not copies but originals. They are one-of-a-kind works of art. Their uniqueness gives them value. In this case, they are worth $66 million. Last, it is worth noticing that as chic as Ms. Picasso's Paris home must certainly be, the pieces that were stolen from her home are far more valuable than the home itself. The contents are worth more than their home.

The same is true of your heart. It has intrinsic value because its Creator is the living God. He dwells there, and His value dwells there too. The content of your heart is the most significant thing you have. Think about it: God, He who hung the clouds and pushes them along on the winds of His breath; God, who created the seen and the unseen; the original musician who conducts symphonies of crickets and lullabies of ocean waves; this very God dwells in your heart.

Your heart is also valuable because it is an original. The eternal God fashioned it to be a one-of-a-kind masterpiece! There is not and will never be another heart like yours. No one has your gifts, talents, experiences, family or influence. Because your heart is unique, you are unique. Your existence on this planet, right now, has eternal significance. You, your heart and everything in it, are a part of God's plan. All creation is waiting expectantly for you to be you.

Come on! Bust on out! The world is waiting.

The richest and wisest man in the world, King Solomon said, "Above all else, guard your heart, for it is the wellspring of life" (Proverbs 4:23 NIV). *Above all else,* Solomon says to guard our hearts. We don't guard trash. We don't protect the ordinary things. We guard that which is valuable. Our hearts are valuable because they are the very sanctuary of God, fashioned to be our forever connection to Him. He values our hearts, and we should too. It's an original!

You have value . . . infinite value. Your heart is proof of that. God created and placed it at the core of who you are. Jesus died for it. And now, you and your heart belong to God's family, the most wealthy and powerful family in the universe. Your heart is your connection to God and that family. It is invaluable. It is your lifeline. Never take Solomon's charge lightly to guard your heart *above all else.*

WELLSPRING OF LIFE

The heart is the place where we experience the full width and depth of life – we dream our wildest dreams, protect our most private secrets and root our deepest loves. Holding such treasures, your heart is not only valuable and purposeful, but it is also vulnerable. It is here that you experience the most intense joy and absorb the most horrific pain. All of the issues of life flow out of the heart. If it matters to you, know that it has flowed through your heart. Your heart processes and records every significant event in your life, both positive and negative:

scarring abuse, tender first love, destructive words and great accomplishment. The human heart can be wounded, seemingly beyond repair. It can be the source of driving conviction, or it can become hard as a stone.

Why would God create the heart to be so tender and yet allow it to be exposed to such an intense variety of life experiences? A fully-lived life requires a fully-experienced life. Without both joy and sorrow, peace and turmoil, happiness and despair, you cannot fully appreciate any one experience. For a life to be fully lived, it must be experienced in every extreme. The extent to which we are capable of experiencing great disappointment and pain is also the extent to which we have the capacity to experience the greatest joy. God wired us for fullness, and our hearts require full exposure for real, authentic life to flow. While we would never choose the extreme moments, they are part of the plan of God.

God designed you to live from your heart. Created to manifest His glory on the earth, you were uniquely made for this moment in time. Hard-wired from the factory of heaven, you were meant to shine. Only when you live life from your heart, embracing all of its experiences, will you experience the width, the depth and the height of this great adventure of God.

As children, we were born with a spiritual compass that knew there was a destination to life – a personal and divine destiny. We knew there was a purpose. And we knew it in our hearts. Back then, life was an adventure. We looked around every corner for the next exciting thing. We lived in wide-eyed wonder of what was next. As adults though, life usually turns into a series of calculated risks. The adventure is removed, and the expectation dies. We rein in our expectations, hopes and dreams. We settle for . . . well . . . less.

We weren't meant to live this way. We weren't meant to live our lives with God as adults. Remember, we are children of God. We were created for adventure. We were intended to be daring, bold, fabulous and remarkable. We were meant to reflect the explosive life and dynamic creativity of our God, our Maker.

Sadly, most of us have grown up and given up. The life we were created for has died because somewhere along the way, we quit living – we stopped being kids. For some, it happened instantly in a traumatic event – abuse, molestation or abandonment. For others, it happened over time. It was slow, almost painless. It wasn't a physical death, but something much more severe . . . spiritual death. However it happened, whenever it happened, whoever or whatever caused it – we died.

How did it happen to you?

When did you change?

How old were you when your heart began to die?

When did you decide it just wasn't worth the risk?

Who or what wounded your heart?

Most people are living, but are not alive. The longest trip in the world is the 18 inches between the head and the heart. It is the distance between merely being alive and actually living. When we live from our heads, everything stops. If the heart and the head never connect, our spiritual life stops. Our hearts are choked by the busyness of our minds. Our spirits are overrun by an onslaught of heart-stopping thoughts. To purely intellectualize life is to die. Knowledge for the sake of knowledge causes spiritual heart attacks.

The symptoms of a spiritual heart attack are devastating. We stop dreaming. We stop praying. We stop believing. We stop hoping. And we stop loving. Instead of embracing life, we analyze it. Instead of pursuing our dreams, we settle for something tolerable and predictable. Instead of searching out our destiny, we choose boredom because it simply makes more sense. It's more logical.

Those 18 inches have been the death of many a life that has disregarded the importance of the heart.

Your past, dreams, wounds, desires, disappointments, mistakes and abuses are integral parts of your heart. Don't run from them any longer. Your heart is the wellspring of life. All of your experiences are the things that have made you, you. **Nothing** in your heart has stunned God or caught Him off guard. **Nothing** in your past, present or future has deterred God from His plan and purpose for you. **Nothing** that you have done or had done to you has disqualified you from service in His Kingdom. NOTHING!

Revisit the dreams of your childhood. Build again, create again, dream again and live again. Go back to that tree house . . . the tree house of your heart. Climb on up to that room built for two. Meet your Maker and learn to live with Him. Dwell with Him in your heart, and then experience the life you were intended to live. A life lived from the Original Sanctuary – your heart.

Endnotes

1 "Sanctuary": Entry from *Webster's II New Riverside Notebook Dictionary, School and Office Edition.* Copyright © 1996 by Houghton Mifflin and *Merriam-Webster's Concise Dictionary.* Copyright © 2006 by Merriam-Webster.

JOURNAL

When did you begin losing your child-like expectation of life?

_____

_____

_____

_____

_____

_____

_____

_____

_____

_____

How did it happen?

_____

_____

_____

_____

_____

_____

_____

JOURNAL

Who or what has wounded your heart?

_____

_____

_____

_____

_____

_____

_____

_____

_____

_____

_____

_____

_____

Do you live life from your head or your heart?

_____

_____

_____

_____

_____

_____

_____

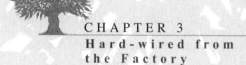

CHAPTER 3
Hard-wired from the Factory

"THE TRAGEDY OF LIFE IS WHAT DIES INSIDE
OF A MAN WHILE HE LIVES."
ALBERT SCHWEITZER

"Our deepest fear is not that we are inadequate.
Our deepest fear is that we are powerful beyond measure.
It is our light, not our darkness, that most frightens us.
We ask ourselves, who am I to be brilliant, gorgeous, talented,
and fabulous? Actually, who are you not to be? You are a child
of God. Your playing small doesn't serve the world. There's
nothing enlightened about shrinking so that other people
won't feel insecure around you. We are all meant to shine,
as children do. We are born to make manifest the glory of God
that is within us. It's not just in some of us, it's in everyone.
And as we let our own light shine, we unconsciously give other
people permission to do the same. As we are liberated from our
own fear, our presence automatically liberates others."

Quoted in the motion picture *Akeelah and the BEE*

 MARC

"The Original U" is a personality test on steroids, and taking it
was one of the best things I have ever done. My friend Paige gave
me the test. She explained the how-to's, and I went to work on a
series of questions. When I finished we totaled the test results and
began to talk about what the test actually meant. As Paige began
explaining my primary personality type a tremendous wave of hope
washed over me. "Marc," she said, "God hard-wired you from the
factory of heaven to be who you are."

Source reference: A Return to Love was originally written by Marianne Williamson."
Quoted in the motion picture Akeelah and the Bee (2006).

*In asking me a series of questions, Paige helped release me
from self-imposed expectations of how my life really should look.
Her words began unhooking me from my own mental matrix of
expectations and stereotypes imposed on me by myself and others.
She made me feel "normal." The more she talked, the better I felt.
With each explanation of my "wiring," hope leaped in my heart.
Maybe she was right. Maybe I'm not the only one who struggles
in the areas that I do.*

*But there was something very familiar about her probing. Her
questions mimicked those that had echoed in my mind my whole
life. From childhood, there had been a voice raising doubts
and uncertainties about who I was and what I should be like.
She continued:*

> *"Have you felt messed up and flawed most of your life?"*
>
> *"Do you wish that you could be less emotional and passionate?"*
>
> *"Do you ever feel like you should have been born during
> a time when things were more wild and adventuresome?"*

*I couldn't believe what I was hearing. Was I dreaming? Was
this lady a bird of a feather that had flocked to me because she
was just as screwed up as me? No, no, she must have been from
God because she read my mail; it was like she had been inside my
head and knew my deepest thoughts and fears. For the first time,
I began to see that maybe, just maybe, I was not as messed up as
I had always believed.*

*As her emotional and spiritual interrogation continued, she
highlighted my strengths and weaknesses and then showed me
how each played a foundational role in who God created me to be.
She even compared my personality traits with those of biblical role*

models like Aaron, John and King David. King David? Are you kidding me? I had been told that I was rebellious and needed to learn to be more common, that I needed to just blend in. And this woman comes along and tells me that I have an emotional and spiritual wiring that resembles that of King David!

In those moments, a new revelation took form in my heart: I express a portion of God's divine nature that no one else will ever be able to manifest on this earth. I am not screwed up. I am unique. What a novel idea. God hard-wired me with core values, strengths, weaknesses and a divine thumbprint, a one-of-a-kind masterpiece equipped to fulfill His ordained assignments for the Kingdom.

And then it hit me like a ton of bricks – God likes who I am. Hold on, rewind that . . . I know He loves and receives me for who I am. After all, God is love; He is supposed to love me. But like me? No one is twisting His arm to like me. But He does. God made me like this, and He likes who I am.

In one fatal swoop, my long-held illusion that God only tolerated me and my antics because He was obligated to was completely demolished. The truth was God uniquely designed me to be in relationship with Him because He likes me. What a difference that made! I had always felt dysfunctional and broken. Finally, I began to realize that God uses broken people like me to accomplish His will and purpose throughout the world.

God is not nearly as interested in fixing me as He is in using me right where I am. He wants me, with all of my stuff, to partner with Him to release His Kingdom in the earth.

Marc

How you start in life is not nearly as important as how you finish. But there is an onslaught of noise that is barking at us, encouraging us to quit. So many voices are shouting messages of disqualification to our hearts, yet God wants us to know that He can use our weaknesses, strengths and personalities to glorify Himself. Have you ever felt trapped in a package of emotions and character flaws that were destined to keep you from being "good enough." Hear us when we say – God loves you and even LIKES you just the way you are.

God doesn't want to change your personality. He is not trying to tame you. He is not trying to break you like you are some out of control horse. In fact, He wants to expand who you are even more. He is calling you out of your box, out of the borders where you are free to be you. This is an invitation to celebrate who you are and who God intended you to be. Outside the box and beyond the border is where God lives. And He is inviting us to come with Him.

He does not want to shut you down. He wants start you up. His deepest desire is to ignite a fire in you that is unlike any other on the planet. Actually, He is trying to reset you to the original hard-wiring that He placed in you from the factory. He is in the business of renewing and restoring the "originality of U."

 DAVID

I'M AN ALIEN!

"Therefore, if anyone is in Christ, he is a new creation; old things have passed away; behold, all things have become new" (2 Corinthians 5:17 NKJV). *When I read this verse it usually makes me feel like an alien. I know that sounds weird. So let me explain. When I accepted Jesus Christ as ruler of my life, I entered a new Kingdom. I received a new life. All things became new. Why then do I so often feel exactly the same as I did before? Screwed up! Goofed up! And emotionally tied up! The confusion comes because the "new nature" mentioned in 2 Corinthians 5:17 is trapped in the same old body. My body looks like I live here, but my insides are from another Kingdom. I AM AN ALIEN!*

My confusion came because I did not understand what was happening in my interior. I now have an internal moral compass steering me one direction and a body, will and emotions that are desperately trying to go another. What is up with that?

You see, I am a three-part person, made up of spirit, soul and body. I AM a spirit. I HAVE a soul. And I LIVE in a body. Say that out loud, "I am a spirit. I have a soul. I live in a body." Three parts, yet one whole.

The spirit is the eternal part of my existence; it is the truest thing about me. My soul, on the other hand, is made up of the mind, will and emotions. The soul is the seat of personality, will, preferences and emotional wiring. Lastly, the body is the package in which I live while visiting this planet. It's my dirt suit.

Now, when I received forgiveness from Christ, my spirit was saved. That's it. Nothing more. Nothing less. The eternal part of me, my spirit, was forever wrapped in the mighty grip of God. However, the rest of me – soul and body – is as lost as it has ever been. My mind, my temperament, habits, mouth, attitudes, character – all lost. That's right . . . all lost!

That explained a lot. Those attitudes and habits that keep popping up are lost. All of those cesspool thoughts that bubble up at the most inopportune times . . . all lost. Those character flaws that I

*have tried so desperately to manage. They're lost. All of these
things are still there because that part of my soul or body is not yet
completely renewed.*

David

When Christ saved us and forgave us, a major overhaul was begun
within us. No longer was there just the selfish soul reigning and
ruling in the body, but the spirit (the eternal part) was alive as well.
Now the soul and spirit occupy the same space. They are both
trapped inside your body, your dirt suit. Because the soul is not yet
completely renewed, it continues to act like it always did, but with
opposition from the spirit. These two natures create an internal tug
of war between what we know in our hearts to be true of our salvation and of what we see in our flesh, attitudes and actions.

The Apostle Paul wrote two-thirds of the New Testament. He was
there when the church was birthed in the early first century and
was the mentor and spiritual father to the early believers. The boy
was a spiritual heavyweight. I would say that Paul had it going on.
Right?

Listen to his personal confession:

*"So I find this law at work: When I want to do good, evil is right
there with me. For in my inner being I delight in God's law; but I
see another law at work in the members of my body, waging war
against the law of my mind and making me a prisoner of the law of
sin at work within my members. What a wretched man I am! Who
will rescue me from this body of death?" (Romans 7:21-24 NIV)*

Can anyone out there relate to our buddy Paul? He understood the
battle between our spirit, soul and body. This struggle between two
worlds – one of the flesh and one of the spirit – explains the Jekyll

and Hyde spirituality that runs rampant in the church. We act all nice and spiritual at church and then open up a brand-new can of road rage on the way to Sunday lunch. We hide and pretend that we are really fine. We cover up the old stuff because we wrongly assume that no one else has any stuff. We pretend because we think we have to. We act like we "get it" when we don't have a clue.

"ALL THINGS HAVE BECOME NEW."

Everything is new, except one thing: our old stuff. We are living in the new Kingdom, but we brought all of our old baggage. When we arrived here, it didn't take long before we learned a new routine of making our baggage look really good. But don't be fooled, it's still old stuff. Most of us have become masters at disguising and hiding our baggage from other people. We may have painted the bags, re-upholstered them and tied scriptures on the handles to make them look better, but the same moldy trash still remains inside.

Please don't get me wrong, life in the new Kingdom is awesome. The salvation of God is the cornerstone of life. His forgiveness of our wretched cesspools is the most marvelous gift He could give. But if you are like us, you are probably frustrated and wondering: If I'm supposed to be new, why do I still have "stuff"? Why didn't God just fix me all at once?

 DAVID

A LETTER FROM DADDY

Several years ago, I went through some intensive counseling for depression and anxiety. As part of this process, my counselor gave me a homework assignment. She asked me to spend some time by myself and ask the Holy Spirit to give me a letter from the Lord. At the outset, I thought that was one of the goofiest, unspiritual things that I had ever been asked to do. Later that week though, I sat down and got quiet, and the Holy Spirit showed up. He began to speak, and I began to write. What came out was this amazing gift:

From the heart of God to me:　　　　　　　　　*Spring - 2000*

Whatever your past has held, whatever family or lack thereof, that you grew up in, whether you were adequately nurtured or abnormally smothered, I am sovereign! The temperament which you were given was given by Me. Your mind and body were given by Me. Whatever deficiencies you <u>perceive</u> in your life . . . trust My sovereignty. Trust My plan.

What you call "baggage," I call ministry tools. What you call "handicaps," I call cords of strength that bind your inadequacies to my boundless resources. One day you will know fully. For now, trust My sovereignty.

Being messed up, goofed up, screwed up, washed up or emotionally thrown up doesn't disqualify you from service and usefulness in My Kingdom. As a matter of fact, I am intensely attracted to weakness and brokenness. Neediness makes you usable. There is a true irony in anointed ministry . . . broken and yet used. Only the truly broken are ever truly used. My own Son was broken badly and yet used eternally.

Your value lies not in what you do, but in what you are. And you are My child! You have endowed abilities and talents given to you out of My resources to complete the tasks that I have set before you. If you are pursuing My plans and My Kingdom, the resources from which you will draw are endlessly Mine. However, if the plans are yours, you are on your own.

You are safely and unchangeably in the grip of the Almighty. You, My dear one, are loved.

The day I received my letter from God changed my life. His truth invaded my lies. His light invaded my darkness. When I heard His voice, I began the process of walking from forgiveness toward freedom.

David

FORGIVEN AND FREE

You are not broken. God is renewing you. He has already forgiven you and is calling you into a destiny of freedom to live as He created you to live. God's forgiveness of sin is a gift. Freedom from the old "stuff," however, is a process we must choose to participate in. Going back to our three-part make up of spirit, soul and body: forgiveness and salvation are for your spirit, freedom is for your soul and body.

The moment you accepted the Father's forgiveness was the beginning of your walk with Christ. In that moment, your spirit's eternal salvation was unshakeable. However, it was not the completed work of God in your life. Salvation is a completed work of Christ. Your salvation will not be completed until your heart stops beating and you are standing in His presence. Your initial saving encounter with God was just the beginning – the beginning of a lifetime of saving and redeeming encounters with the Father.

The purpose and plan of the gospel is for the working out of your salvation (Philippians 2:12). When we whole-heartedly chase new life in Christ, the Holy Spirit changes us from glory to glory (2 Corinthians 3:18). When we agree to the process of freedom, life becomes a series of encounters with God's grace and mercy. In this "working out," unknown areas of bondage are saved and restored. Don't look at this like it's a systematic process. Look at it as an adventure.

Right now, there are territories in your heart, mind and emotions that are under bondage to lies. The enemy has placed signs there that read, "No trespassing." You have lies that have claimed territory in your heart like an old fashioned Oklahoma land rush. He is riding through land that he does not own and is sticking flags (lies) in the ground like he owns the place. But it is not his land. He is a squatter.

The truth of God can invade those areas and colonize them with unchanging principles that will set you free. *"Praise the LORD, O my soul, and forget not all his benefits – who forgives all your sins and heals all your diseases, who redeems your life from the pit and crowns you with love and compassion"* (Psalm 103:2-4 NIV). Freedom is available from your past, present, mistakes, choices, abusers, addictions and afflictions.

Years ago, I heard a fascinating story about the great illusionist, Harry Houdini. The story revolved around a challenge Houdini accepted to attempt an escape from a locked jail cell. After being confined to the cell, Houdini began his escape. After several hours of unsuccessful effort, Houdini was exasperated, embarrassed and defeated. He sat down on the floor and leaned up against the door . . . the weight of his body pushed it open. The door had been unlocked the entire time. Houdini was free and didn't know it. He had feverishly tried to pick a lock that wasn't locked at all.

Most of the people we meet these days are living in a Houdini-like frustration. They live in what seems to be locked cells when in actuality, they are free. Just like Houdini, they are too busy trying to pick the lock to realize that the door isn't locked at all. In a nutshell, they are forgiven but they are not free. WHY? Most of them are trying too hard to pick the lock with good works, more spiritual information, conference hopping and church attendance.

Sadly, most believers assume that God's only interest in their lives was in offering them an exemption from an eternity in hell. Accepting this partial truth has banished them to a life of plodded, lifeless mediocrity in which their next great event in life is death. When we believe life holds no significance for us, our hearts die. While our spirits are sealed by forgiveness and expect a future hope of heaven, our souls and bodies die, trapped in an unintended bondage. We are forgiven, but not free.

Forgiveness and freedom are two completely different things. Forgiveness comes from our belief and acceptance of Jesus; freedom is found in complete surrender to Him. Forgiveness of our sins is the eternal redemption of our spirits, promising our places in heaven. Freedom is the present reality of our minds, wills, emotions and bodies being released and restored to God's original intent.

It is entirely possible to be forgiven of your sin but completely bound and enslaved to your past, your sin, your addiction, your abuser and even your own ideas. Freedom is an expression and experience of God on this planet, today. True freedom is the state in which heaven invades earth and we begin to experience the benefits of our forgiveness NOW.

So we ask you, are you forgiven or are you free?

A SHORT TRIP

Since forgiveness and freedom are two different things, there must be a way to go from forgiveness to freedom. How do we get there?

The answer is simple: repentance. Don't overreact or pull back from this word. Stick with us . . .

"So here's what I want you to do, God helping you: Take your everyday, ordinary life . . . and place it before God as an offering. Embracing what God does for you is the best thing you can do for him. Don't become so well-adjusted to your culture that you fit into it without even thinking. Instead, fix your attention on God. You'll be changed from the inside out. Readily recognize what he wants from you, and quickly respond to it. Unlike the culture around you, always dragging you down to its level of immaturity, God brings the best out of you, develops well-formed maturity in you." (Romans 12:1-2 MSG)

In this passage, Paul describes repentance. When he wrote this letter to the Romans in the first century, the common understanding of the Greek word for repentance was not "try harder to do something good." No, the idea is to simply to *change your mind*. We must begin the process of changing our paradigms of thought through which we perceive life, love, God, truth, others and the world around us.

Changing the way we think and what we are thinking about is the first step in renewing our mind. Step out of your culture for a moment – the culture of religion, tradition and even of your own thinking. We want to help you change your mind about your heart. Look into the timeless truths of scripture and change you mind about how you have seen your heart in the past. Understand and embrace it the way God intended.

A GLORIOUS HEART

Romans 3:23 says, *". . . all have sinned and fall short of the glory of God"* (NIV). Typically, we use this verse as an evangelistic hammer to scripturally prove that folks who don't know Jesus are a bunch of misfits who missed the call of God for their lives. Their ignorance is a swing and a miss attempt at spirituality because they have completely failed to please Him.

Maybe this idea of "falling short" has contributed to the belief that God gives His grace and mercy reluctantly. Many people have embraced a mental image of God kicking the dirt and saying, "Okay . . . I guess I'll let you into heaven." What a half-empty, deficient view of God that is!

Notice, the writer did not say that we have fallen short of the forgiveness, grace, mercy, goodness or love of God. That is not the message of the gospel. Our salvation goes much deeper than forgiveness, grace and mercy. It bores down to our hearts, drilling toward complete restoration. We have fallen short of "glory." The goal of the gospel is glory!

Romans 3:23 does not say that God, in His pity, will return us to some pseudo-human, vegetable-like existence: sin-free, but still lacking. Nope. God's deposit of grace goes far beyond the removal of our sin debt. The forgiveness of our sin is just the staging area for God's full purpose in our lives, namely, the return to our originally-intended home. We were saved for a trip to a place even greater and grander than forgiveness and acceptance. We were destined for original glory.

There was, and is, an original beauty and rhythm created by God in the Garden of Eden. God wants to restore you to His intended glory for you. Your heart is not so much bad as it is broken. Theologians and preachers often remind us of our sinful nature, our depravity, our "bad" heart. This "original sin" speaks of when the rhythm went bad, setting us up for lives of

helplessness, sin and disobedience. And while it is important
that we understand this truth, we need to hear something from
the heart of God . . .

Before dysfunction, there was perfect function.

*Before our hearts beat with irregularity, there was a regular,
glorious rhythm.*

Before separation, there was a sanctuary.

Before the deafening silence, there was raucous laughter.

*Before Adam and Eve covered with loin clothes, they took an
evening stroll with God.*

*Before we saw God only as holy, righteous, just, unreachable,
unapproachable, illusive and distant, He was Daddy!*

God created us to be inhabitants of the original sanctuary.
When sin cut off our access, He sent Jesus to restore us to the
Garden state. We are saved to thrive in intimate relationship
with our Creator God . . . our Daddy. We were not only saved
for the forgiveness of our sin and the promise of heaven, but
for His glory to overtake us *right now.* We were saved for His
Kingdom to come in our lives today.

Weakness welcomes the release of God's magnified strength
in our lives. Struggles and wounds are the building materials
God uses to display His glory in and through us. Your unique
personality displays the creative deposit of God in your life. So
don't run from your weaknesses, struggles, pain or personality.

Face them head on. Embrace them. Learn to accept and celebrate them. They will make grace all the more amazing.

God is not looking for perfect lives and hearts, but for obedient, submissive and grateful ones. Learn to enjoy the *working out of your salvation* (Philippians 2:12). It may be messy, ugly and even bloody, but it is glorious. Your Daddy is waiting to release His glory in and through you, tapping into the unique person He created you to be.

Don't listen to the condemning words rattling around in your head, telling you that you are disqualified or worthless. Your heart is a sanctuary, and you do belong to God's Kingdom. Discover the rhythm, the original perfection of your heart. Dream about your Daddy and imagine just how glorious He is. He placed His glory in you through Christ.

There is glory in your heart. There is beauty in your heart. There is purity in your heart. You were hard-wired from the factory with a divine and heavenly expression that all of creation longs to see. So stop apologizing and start living!

JOURNAL

_____

_____

_____

_____

_____

_____

_____

_____

_____

_____

_____

_____

_____

_____

_____

_____

_____

_____

_____

_____

JOURNAL

CHAPTER 4
I'm Fine . . . Really

"DENIAL IS THE WORST SORT OF HEART DISEASE KNOWN TO MANKIND. IN DENYING THE IMAGE DISPLAYED IN THE MIRROR WE UNKNOWINGLY DISMISS FREEDOM AND CEASE TO EXIST." ANONYMOUS

MARC

Most of my life, I have been defined by old clichés. When my teen-age friends were influencing my bad attitude, my parents quoted, "Birds of a feather flock together." My parents insisted that I had serious issues with my choice of friends and had obvious concerns about where that could lead. People always seemed to label me and define my boundaries. It was a box of rules and regulations, do's and don'ts. The most quoted saying over my life has to be: "Marc, you are like a bull in a china shop!"

Even as a boy, I was aggressive and loud. I was constantly being accused of being too strong with my words and out there with my actions. Just thinking about the words makes me want to scream. "Marc, you are too loud . . . too rowdy . . . too sensitive . . . too emotional . . . blah, blah, blah." The only thing those biting words accomplished was to communicate that I was messed up and had little hopes of ever fitting in. The phrases stuck to me like a bumper sticker declaring to the world that I wasn't normal. I believed that something was unchangeably wrong with who I was and how I was wired.

After my conversion to Christianity, most of the Body of Christ seemed to echo the painful voices of my childhood. Though Jesus had rescued me, people kept repeating the message I had heard my whole life – something is wrong with who I am. "Marc, you can't say those kinds of things in church. You need to be more reverent. You don't always have to be so honest in front of a group."

Early on, this confused me. Are you kidding me? I thought God knew all my thoughts and the motives behind each word that I shared. Why were people so afraid of my transparency? Were they that uncomfortable dealing with real issues? Was I the only one thinking these thoughts?

As a new believer, I desperately wanted to be obedient to the voice of God. I figured that maybe they were right. Maybe I was too rebellious and needed to change. With no other place to call home and no one to affirm who I was, I submitted and accepted the lie. Like a sheep led to its slaughter, I walked into the castrating chutes and allowed the institution to spiritually emasculate me. I blended in and died to who I was.

I began to lie to myself and others. Any time I was asked how I was doing, I simply replied, "I'm fine, how are you?"

Marc

A good friend once told me, "David, the worst person you can ever lie to is yourself." In every area of life – spiritual, emotional, financial, physical – I have found this to be very true. It is dangerous to live a lie! The Bible even tells us so: *"If we say that we have fellowship with Him, and walk in darkness, we lie and do not practice the truth"* (1 John 1:6 NKJV). For us to live in untruth is to walk in spiritual and emotional darkness.

A healthy and godly life is one lived in the light. *"But if we walk in the light as He is in the light, we have fellowship with one another, and the blood of Jesus Christ His Son cleanses us from all sin"* (1 John 1:7 NKJV). The promise of this verse is that if we are living in the light, horizontal relationships with other people will be authentic fellowship as God intended. Secondly, living in the light cleanses from all sin. It sounds to me like we should be attracted to the light and truth-telling and run from the lies of the dark. Unfortunately, most of us have learned to live in a twisted

reality where darkness is comforting and exposure to the light
is terrifying.

I believe the primary reason we prefer darkness over light is that we
don't really believe Jesus when He said, *". . . the truth will set you
free"* (John 8:32 NIV). Oh, we would say that we believe the Bible
and the teachings of Jesus, but our actions speak much louder than
most of our words. We have applied this truth to our salvation, but
have forgotten it when it comes to our daily lives. Not only does the
truth set us free to inherit heaven, but it also waits to bring heaven
down to life on earth.

Jesus' words apply to every area of our lives – our emotions,
finances and relationships. His Word is *always* true, all the time,
in every situation and circumstance. His truth can set us free,
if we will let it. By submitting to the principle of stating and
acknowledging truth, we will live more freely than we ever
dreamed or imagined.

What's holding us back from living in light and freedom? Why does
the thought of living transparently before God and others terrify us?
Why does it make us squirm in our seats when others share their
deep pain and failure?

IS IT WORTH THE RISK?

> *"We long to be known and we fear it like nothing else. Most people
> live with subtle dread that one day they will be discovered for who
> they really are and the world will be appalled."*
> Sacred Romance (John Eldredge / Brent Curtis / T. Nelson - 1997)

For most of us, the greatest risk we will ever take is opening
our heart to another human being. The thought of pouring out
our innermost failures, dreams and hopes brings on a flood of

emotions, primarily fear. Most married couples that we meet have very little conversation, if any, with their spouses about their fears, hurts, dreams and struggles. When we expose what has been hidden, there is an unknown factor of how others (including God) will respond.

Unfortunately, most of us have experienced rejection or isolation when we revealed our weaknesses and sins to other believers. Opening up, exposing yourself for who you really are, has proven to be a risky proposition that could result in you being shot down, wounded or maybe even disassociated. If you have seen this happen to someone else, you may be thinking, *If they treated him like that, what would they do to me if they really knew me? Surely, they would reject me or use my deficiencies against me.*

Why should typical believers hope for living in the light when they see other people ostracized for being less than perfect? No wonder transparency is so uncommon among Christians. We shouldn't be surprised that church attendance is dropping in this country . . . an army that shoots its own wounded doesn't recruit many new soldiers. This is not a disease in the church but rather in our individual hearts. The church isn't broken, it's just full of broken people.

What we often fail to realize, though, is that most of those doing the "wounding" are lost and wounded themselves. Hurt people hurt people. Frightened people frighten people. The fear of being exposed is a driving force in the body of Christ. The pain in our own hearts and lives drives us to unknowingly shut down others around us from reaching for freedom. *If I can't have it, they can't have it.* This fear of being found out is so strong that it is actually greater than our desire to be free. Ouch! The truth stings!

We have come to realize that people who have not experienced personal freedom outside of their salvation tend to push their bondage on other believers. Even those who have known freedom are sometimes timid in offering that same freedom to others because of the ever-present threat of alienation or misunderstanding.

So, in the family of God, where our sins and weaknesses should be most welcome, there is tremendous risk involved in stepping into the light. As much as we want raw, transparent honesty, we all know that it is much easier to just keep pretending that we are someone else. Keep the truth inside. Continue the posing game. Fake it. Walk in darkness. Pretend. Blend in. Just be beige.

But posing is not living, is it? Pretending to be something we are not only leads to a lonely life of shadows and straw where nothing is ever truly real. While our façades may have the appearance of "religious goodness," there is no real life, passion or power behind it. Walking in the shadows, nothing is ever truly fulfilling, pure, noble or honorable. We look good on the outside, but inside, we are empty.

One thing that is certain, when nothing is risked, nothing is gained. Let's face it. Our fear of being "found out" has us bound and gagged. Without the prospect of a large pay off, most of us will never risk revealing ourselves. Going back to Jesus' promise of the truth setting us free, our question to you is: Is finding freedom worth the risk of stepping into the light? Are you tired of your counterfeit life? Are you ready to be known and loved for who you really are?

DAVID

SEEK AND GO HIDE

One hot Saturday morning, my then four-year-old son, Gibson, and I were playing the favorite age-old game, Hide and Go Seek. We played the game in a large, open portion of a local park. I went first, closing my eyes, counting to ten (about five times) and waiting for him to hide. When I looked up, I noticed his blond-haired head exposed over the top of a park bench about 75 feet away. I grinned and chuckled, thinking he didn't know that I could see him. You know how kids are – they think that if they can't see you, then surely you can't see them.

What I quickly realized, though, was that Gibson was not that clueless. He was fully aware that I could see him. To his delight, he saw me looking at him. Not only could I see his eyes peering over the back of the park bench, I could hear him giggling all the way across that playground.

*He knew that I could see him. He wanted me to see him. His plan was to be partially visible and then watch me find him. The goal of the game was not to hide so well that he **wouldn't** be found . . . it was to hide so that he **would.***

Later that evening I was studying in my office and the Lord brought to my mind the picture of me and Gibson playing in the park. I wrote these thoughts in my journal:

> *Gibson longs for me to recognize his presence and his absence. God designed him to desire the security of April and me. His security is affirmed by our knowing who he is and where he is. He loves the joy of being found. He loves knowing that we know where he is.*

I need security just as much as Gibson does. That thought doesn't feel masculine at all. Deep down, that makes me feel very weak and needy. Why do I feel that way? I have been infected by a culture that defines people from the outside, in. I teach my son to do the exact opposite. But I seem unable to live this out. I operate from a decidedly different paradigm than Gibson does. Somewhere along the way, I stopped finding joy in being found. I don't like being looked for, much less discovered.

"Hide and Go Seek?" or "Seek and Go Hide?" Which game am I playing?

God, I need help and deliverance. I seek it. I read about it. I hear about it. And instead of going after it, I just get scared and go hide. I seek it, find it and then run from it . . .

David

What is it about being a Christian that makes it so hard to be genuine? Is it fear? Emotional protection? A competitive need to be better than others? Instead of showing ourselves freely, we have taken to burying ourselves behind masks of pleasantries and surface relationships, hoping never to be found out.

Whatever the reason, most of us have lost sight of the need for transparency, taking comfort in the art of posing. Now, we may not set out to pose, but the fact remains that being genuine with people requires special focus, hard work and, quite frankly, the hand of God.

Authentic life is contradictory to our nature. Remember those two opposing and conflicting natures residing within you? The spirit

that God breathed life into wants to be genuine and authentic.
But the soul, that old nature that is still being changed and saved,
is terrified. Remember: You are a spirit. You have a soul. And
you live in a body. Your "three-part person" is alive and well.
And the battle is on!

To give into the fear of exposure robs us of significant relationships
and dooms us to lifeless, impotent religion. On the other hand,
taking the risk of pulling off the masks, opens us up to a whole
new world of relational possibilities. The impulse we follow will
determine how all of our relationships and spirituality play out
in life.

When the joy of being found is lost, we trade a fun game of Hide
and Go Seek for the self-preserving game of Seek and Go Hide.
Though we claim to seek after God, we are actually hiding from
Him, others and real life.

JOURNAL

Do you remember when the paradigm shifted for you?

_____

_____

_____

_____

_____

_____

_____

Where did you lose the joy of being found?

_____

_____

_____

_____

_____

_____

_____

Who betrayed your confidence?

_____

_____

_____

_____

_____

JOURNAL

Have you ever had joy?

_____

_____

_____

_____

_____

_____

_____

What is the root of your fear?

_____

_____

_____

_____

_____

_____

_____

_____

_____

_____

_____

_____

_____

CHAPTER 4 1/2
Naked or Neck-ed

"EVERYBODY IS NORMAL UNTIL YOU GET
TO KNOW THEM." JOHN ORTBERG

DAVID

I grew up in a small town in east Texas – watermelons, black-eyed peas, dove hunting, family reunions and Friday night football games. Most of the family from my father's side, aunts, uncles and cousins (hundreds of them), are scattered all over that part of the state.

East Texans are known for their colorful sayings and colloquialisms. One of my favorites is a home-spun definition for the word <u>naked</u>. While "naked" means you don't have any clothes on, "neck-ed" means you don't have any clothes on . . . and you're up to something.

David

"Now the serpent was more crafty than any of the wild animals the Lord God had made. He said to the woman, 'Did God really say, "You must not eat from any tree in the Garden"?' . . . When the woman saw that the fruit of the tree was good for food and pleasing to the eye, and also desirable for gaining wisdom, she took some and ate it. She also gave some to her husband, who was with her, and he ate it. Then the eyes of both of them were opened, and they realized they were naked; so they sewed fig leaves together and made coverings for themselves. Then the man and his wife heard the sound of the LORD God as he was walking through the garden in the cool of the day, and they hid from the LORD God among the trees of the garden. But the LORD God called to the man, 'Where are you?' He answered, 'I heard you in the garden, and I was afraid because I was naked; so I hid'"

(Genesis 3:1, 6-10 NIV).

In the Garden of Eden, Adam and Eve took the maiden voyage into sin and selfishness. And after they disobeyed God, what was the first thing they did? They hid.

All along, they had been naked, but suddenly, they were neck-ed. When God came looking for His companions to stroll with in the afternoon, they weren't there. They were up to something. Their sin had caused a separation, a break, an embarrassment. After years of living in the openness of a relationship with God, their sin drove them into hiding.

In Genesis 3:9, God asked Adam and Eve, "Where are you?" That's an interesting question for a God who knows everything. Don't start thinking that God lost them like you lose your car keys. No, God didn't lose Adam and Eve. They lost Him. The reason God had to ask, "Where are you?" is that they didn't realize they had lost Him, yet. God was trying to help them establish where they were in relationship with Him. They had stepped out of His daily presence and thus instantly found themselves lost.

Adam and Eve hid, thinking that was their only means of survival. They reasoned that by hiding, God would lose them and their sin would somehow be overlooked. However, God never lost them; they lost Him.

When Adam realized that his disobedience was found out, he could have confessed his weakness, sin and disobedience. But instead of returning to God to walk with Him the way he had done before so that their relationship could be restored, he chose to walk away.

In the moment that Adam was exposed, why did hiding make so much sense to him? Why does it make so much sense to us when the truth of who we are is revealed? Pain, sin and separation always drive us into hiding. Instead of coming out of the bushes and exposing ourselves to the One who made us, loves us, understands us and can help us, we run for cover. We have been convinced by our culture, other people, the evil one and religion that hiding is holy.

Hiding is not holy but it is instinctive. It is somehow ingrained in how we relate to God and others. It has been the modus operandi of the human race since Adam and Eve sewed those first fig leaves together. Duck and cover. Grin and bear it. We all have done it. Exposure to us has become an enemy, not an antidote. Even though this passage in Genesis records an account of what happened a long time ago, history does tend to repeat itself.

A MODERN DAY GARDEN

When we are with other believers, we play this "holy" game especially well, don't we? You know how it goes: We go to church, Bible study or some kind of ministry function, and we are hurt, depressed, despairing, guilt-ridden, hopeless, mourning . . . fill in your own blank. From the deepest places in our hearts, we hope that all of this God-talk would be true. Deep down, we just want to be forgiven and free. We would give anything for freedom. What a relief it would be just to be able to breathe again! How much would we pay just for an accepting wink from the Savior?

This is the condition we are in when we meet with other Christians. We are seekers, looking for truth, vital relationships and fellowship. We want it ALL. But to get it, we have to risk rejection and expose what is really in our hearts. So what do we do? We run and hide. We head for the bushes instead of the center of the garden. We say we want freedom. We say we want healing. We say we want reality to exist in the light. But when we have the chance to gain these things, ironically, we frantically run from them. All the while

God is calling, "Where are you, _____?" We are the ones who are lost.

DAVID

MY BONANZA FANTASY

As a kid, one of my favorite television shows was Bonanza. *I loved every minute of every episode. When the music started and the picture of the map began to burn, I would put on my cowboy Cartwright clothes and settle in for another adventure. I felt like I was part of the Cartwright family – Adam, Ben, Hoss, Little Joe, Hop Sing the cook and me! I wanted to live on the Ponderosa ranch with them. I wanted to be in the fights, shoot a lever action rifle, help the widows and put the bad guys in jail.*

My favorite character was Little Joe, played by Michael Landon. More than anything, I wanted to be Little Joe Cartwright. I wanted his paint horse. I wanted his flat-top, low-profile cowboy hat and green shirt. I wanted to wear the high-water khaki pants with the pointed cowboy boots. My parents actually have a picture of me dressed up just like Little Joe Cartwright. Stop laughing . . . I looked good!

A few years ago, April and I met some friends in Lake Tahoe, Nevada for a vacation. While driving around the lake one day, I saw a sign that read: "Bonanza-TV Show Filming Location – Visitors Welcome!" As soon as I read that sign, I whipped the rental car down the little dirt road. This was it. A dream of my childhood was about to be realized. The Ponderosa Ranch was just around the bend.

What I found at the end of that road, devastated my childhood dream. My dream had under-delivered. The Ponderosa Ranch wasn't real at all. The Cartwright ranch house was just a front with no back. It was only a prop. It wasn't even big. Four grown men couldn't have lived there. It was tiny! The barn, the town store, the livery stable . . . everything was fake. It looked like the real thing from the outside, but there was absolutely nothing inside. It was a one-dimensional set – authentic and real from one perspective, but empty from every other angle. The Ponderosa Ranch was a fake. And Little Joe was no longer my hero!

David

Do you ever feel like your life is a prop from a television show – perfectly designed to create the illusion of reality, but empty inside? As long as your friends and family look at it from the right angle, everything looks great. But you know the truth . . . behind the scenes, it's far from great. If anyone were able to get close enough, they would see straight through the façade.

Being truthful is hard. Sadly enough, the only time our human nature encourages us to be honest is when we get caught doing something. You know . . . neck-ed. Even then, sometimes it is difficult to admit shortcomings and be transparent. It is so much easier to keep everything a secret and pretend we are something we are not. The danger is that if these areas are kept in the dark, they become inhabitable by the enemy.

Our sinful nature (our flesh) leads us to protect ourselves rather than accept vulnerability. That nature strives for the *ideal* rather than the *real.* The problem is the ideal is a fake – a movie prop. There is no substance behind it. It's nothing more than a counterfeit life, a deception. What is real is our sinful natures and God's grace. Our flesh may not be pretty, but at least it is honest. And God's grace, well, it is enough to cover all of our un-prettiness.

Like we said before, we are in a battle – a battle between old stuff and new stuff. The new man requires life from the Spirit. The old man requires life from the flesh. The new requires truth, reality and light to flourish while the old man still wants to hide. Our flesh will always be horrified by exposure and vulnerability. Yet true life *requires* exposure for freedom to flourish.

This internal tug-of-war of pretending versus transparency defeats many good men and women who desire a different kind of life. We don't intend to be fake. It just kind of happens. Transparency is the only cure for this seemingly terminal existence. Real transparency is the one thing that can crack our façades and remove our false fronts. The vacancy created by an open, honest confession will become the new habitation of the Spirit of God. Only the presence of God in our lives can chip away at the hardness of our hearts and remove pride so that His freedom can enter in. True confessions create a vacancy in our hearts. The vacancy can then be occupied by the Spirit of God.

ADJUSTING THE VEIL

One of the greatest leaders in the Bible learned first hand the consequences of pretending. Exodus 34 lays out the fascinating story of Moses' summons to the Mountain of God to receive a replacement copy of the Ten Commandments. (He had broken the first set in a fit of anger at the Israelites.) For forty days and nights, Moses lived on that mountain in the presence of God.

Following that glory-filled encounter with the Almighty, Moses returned to the Israelite camp with his face glowing with the *shekinah* glory of God. Unassuming and unsuspecting at first, Moses agreed to veil his face because the people could not handle looking at him with the new aura shining from his countenance. With the veil in place, Moses went about his daily tasks.

This is where the story gets interesting. 2 Corinthians 3:13 goes on to explain that Moses, " . . . *put a veil over his face to keep the Israelites from gazing at it while the radiance was fading away"* (NIV). Interesting, isn't it? Moses, the leader of the entire Israelite nation, faked it in front of the very people he was leading. Something in him desperately needed attention or validation. He wanted to know that he was important, and he was willing to fake it to feel the buzz.

Somewhere along the way, Moses saw his reflection in the river and said, "Wow! I look good!" He started to believe that his face-lift had something to do with him. Moses' personal, self-edifying and self-projected image to the people became paramount. His glory rose above the glory of God. His own name and renown became the desire of his heart. Proud of what he used to have and flaunting it as if he still had it, he may as well have stuck out his tongue and sang the taunting childhood song, "I have something you don't have."

What is most fascinating (and convicting) about this story is that when God's glory disappeared, Moses' ego re-appeared . . . on steroids. Although the visible glory of God had departed from Moses' face, he continued to live behind the veil. Why? Most likely, his human nature kicked in: pride, self-righteousness and an insatiable need for validation. Whatever his core character issues, though, the fact is that he continued to live behind the veil long after the glory of God had departed from his face.

Even when he no longer needed the veil, Moses went about his duties within the camp wearing it. The glory of a previous encounter with God had worn off, yet there he sat, looking like he looked before. And nobody knew. No one suspected or accused him of claiming to be something he wasn't. Moses pulled off the charade. No one knew the truth . . . except Moses.

Our hearts always know when we are pretending. Our hearts always know when we are faking it. Our hearts always know when we are hiding something.

The story of Moses' veil may be the first recorded account of a grown man "posing" in the church – pretending to be religious, holy or godly when what is going on inside is far from that. Don't sit there all smug, innocent and self-righteous. Millions of men and women have played this same game of religious duck-and-cover. Remember: History repeats itself, doesn't it?

Most of us have perfected the art of appearing religious. Religion is one of the strongest drugs on the planet. Once we get drawn into the charade, the pretension of perfection, before we know it, we are addicted. Life goes on, but the living stops.

Week after week, year after year, people go to churches and Christian gatherings. Sadly though, many never get the full-flavored taste of the life that Jesus died for. Most of us opt to manage our behavior and image rather than expose our hearts. And it breaks the heart of God. The Kingdom of God is bursting at the seams with religion-addicted pretenders. Are you one of them?

A SLICE OF LIFE

My devotional life is non-existent. Accountability is a joke. My house is in an uproar, and my marriage feels more like sharing a cell with another prisoner than a cherished and loving partnership. Being at home is so hard and depressing . . . I'd rather be at the deer lease (or the mall). The last time I really felt passionate about life was when my son caught a fly ball in his T-ball game.

Where is the joy, peace, patience, gentleness and self-control I am supposed to have? If I have the Holy Spirit inside of me, where is His fruit? I feel so dry and lifeless. In a word, my life is like a desert.

But when Sunday rolls around, things have to look different. We have survived the week, and it is time for church. Somehow, I miraculously manage to get my family out of bed, cleaned up and in the car. We argue all the way there, but as soon as we get out of the car, we look different.

The first person I see that asks, "How are you?" I answer like I always do – "Fine."

Liar! You're not *fine* . . . you're not even remotely *fine*. You can't spell *f-i-n-e*. You couldn't find *fine* if it hit you in the face. In fact, the truth be told, you are a mess! And another weekend match of verbal volleyball has you stiff-arming everyone you meet with your antiseptic *"fine."*

It is just so easy to do, isn't it? You may as well be Moses, adjusting your veil to make sure it hides the real you. *Fine.* You respond. You don't even know why you say it. It's almost uncontrollable. Ingrained. Instinctive. Programmed.

In your defense, though, who are you going to tell? Another Christian? I don't think so. How absurd would that be? They might assume that you were needy or something . . . you can't let that happen. They might actually listen to you and pray for you.

Heaven forbid, they might just minister to you. Good night!
Wouldn't that be horrible!

DAVID

MY COMING OUT PARTY

*Okay, I will tell the truth. I have lived this story a thousand
times. I have been "fine" most of my life. On the worst days, I
was just fine. And of course, on the best days, I was fine too. But
one day, everything changed.*

*I was teaching a large class at our church. I had taught this group
for several years. Known for using creative teaching methods, I
had developed a reputation as a good communicator and teacher.
On this particular Sunday, though, I was bone dry. I was in the
worst depression that I had ever experienced: hopeless, lifeless,
dead from the neck down. Despite my deadness, I was determined
to do the godly thing and teach these people . . . and I was going
to be good.*

*Psalm 122 was the passage that day. As I read the passage, the
Holy Spirit began to do something in my heart. "I rejoiced with
those who said to me, 'Let us go to the house of the Lord'" (verse
1, NIV). What a lie. I didn't want to be there any more than I
wanted a prostate exam.*

*I stayed focused and continued reading in verses 6-7: "Pray
for the peace Jerusalem: 'May those who love you be secure.
May there be peace within your walls and security within your
citadels'" (NIV).*

*Secure? Peace within your walls? These words made me crumble
on the inside. I had no peace. I had no security. My citadel was*

just a pup tent. I was dying on the inside, and no one knew it. I couldn't pretend any longer. I took off my veil.

I closed my Bible. Dead-faced, lifeless and heartsick, I looked into the faces of the hundred or so people who sat in front of me. "I have nothing for you today. I cannot do this. I am in the worst depression and funk of my whole life. If someone doesn't pray for me, I may die!"

The room went dead silent. The class didn't know if I was kidding or serious. Was I creatively making a point or was I really that messed up? After what seemed like a lifetime, Steve, a friend from my Thursday morning men's group, stood up. He made his way from the rear of the room, walked up to me, put his hands on me and began to pray.

As he prayed, I began to weep. Others got up and joined in praying. The room began to spin. My heart began to race. I started to sweat. I thought, "What did I just do?" I am the teacher who is supposed to be fine. I should have it all together. How did I lose control that quickly?

*I never taught that day. It was the best lesson that I **never** taught. The class and I would never be the same. That day was a new beginning for that group of people. We stopped hiding and began to tell the truth. Instead of posing and pretending, we began having real conversations about real things . . . from our hearts. Over the next few weeks, countless people told me that they, too, struggled with depression, anxiety and emotional issues. They had also struggled alone. They were so relieved to know that they were not alone . . . and so was I.*

I would love to tell you that I received instant healing from depression, but it didn't happen that way. That day was the beginning of a journey, a process that led to my healing from a life-long battle with depression. After coming out of the dark, I confronted some of the deepest things in my heart face-to-face, and with the help of a gifted counselor and some strong prayer warriors, I was set free, but almost 3 years later.

The depression has not returned. At the time of this writing, I have been depression-free for more than five years. The day I quit pretending and performing was the day I left my bondage and began walking toward a promise of wholeness and freedom.

What about you? Are you running? Are you pretending? Are you keeping up appearances? Are you fine?

When I was in elementary school, our neighborhood was filled with boys. We were always warring, throwing or launching something into the air. At the epicenter of such energy and freshly-released testosterone, things tended to get broken: a window knocked out with a golf ball, a steel trash can destroyed by an airborne bicycle, and yes, we even tagged a few cars with a water-soaked Nerf football.

At the sound of breaking glass, yelling adults or mangled metal, as soon as one of us realized what we had done, the silence was broken with a loud, "RUN!!!" And we always did, every one of us. I'm 44 years old now, and my first instinct is still to run. When I was younger, I really thought that by this point in my life, the childish tendency would be over. But it's not. Anytime I mess up, the first thing I want to do is get out of there, cover it up. These days, I'm not dealing with broken windows and crumpled up trash cans. What I run from is my recurring habitual sin, greed, selfishness, fear of men, distorted images of God and repeated, ugly attitudes.

The last few years of my life have changed a few things. I have learned how to take off my mask. Now I have more reasons to stay put than run. God's mercy is vast enough to cover my sin. His mercy and restoration are greater than my fear of exposure. God has given me some really good friends, my "Garden Friends." They know my stuff, accept me just as I am, but won't allow me to stay there. These five guys (Jimmy, Paulie, Jay, Richard and Marc) have exhorted and encouraged me to be everything the Father says that I am. We have learned together that pretending is bondage, but honesty is freedom.

My friends can be so gracious to me because they too have eaten at God's all-you-can-eat grace buffet. We have all smelled our cesspools and then immediately whiffed the overcoming grace of God. Owning up to that need, coming together with the desire to walk in the light, has created a place of grace where we can retreat. This is the place where we can be sick and tired of being sick and tired. A place where we find healing. It is the place that we enter the Original Sanctuary of our hearts. We are friends sharing the same tree house.

David

Are you looking for such a place? If you don't long to be completely known and completely accepted, then you aren't ready for life as God intended. Until you are sick and tired of being sick and tired, your life is not likely to change. If you want out of the dead religious cycle of posing, the antidote is transparency.

We *need* to stop hiding. We *have* to stop hiding.

Now, don't think we are saying that everyone you meet needs to know your life struggles. Please, don't confess your deepest wounds to the sacker at the grocery store. It is not prudent or wise to always say everything that you are thinking. What we are trying to communicate is that your life will not always be wonderfully bubbly and barrels of fun, so don't act like it is.

Drop your veil. Expose your struggles: depression, fear, sin, attitudes, addictions, relational dysfunction, your past and your dreams. You know . . . the stuff in your heart. You will probably feel like you have on a hospital gown with the whole world following you down the hall. Try it anyway. Risk it. Go ahead, get naked!

The life God wants for you – the life you crave deep down inside – cannot be lived in private. It cannot be faked or packaged. You cannot pretend to have all of the answers and hide your sin and shortcomings. You can continue to pretend and hide, but your life and heart will never be changed.

True, abundant, authentic life doesn't exist behind high-glossed reputations. It starts with honesty, and it must live in the light of truth. "You shall know the truth and the truth shall set you free."

Naked or neck-ed? You decide.

JOURNAL

_____

_____

_____

_____

_____

_____

_____

_____

_____

_____

_____

_____

_____

_____

_____

_____

_____

_____

_____

_____

_____

_____

_____

JOURNAL

CHAPTER 5
It's Just A Thought

"MORE LIFE MAY TRICKLE OUT OF A MAN THROUGH THOUGHT THAN THROUGH A GAPING WOUND." THOMAS HARDY

MARC

AN UNFORGETTABLE WHIFF

In the rural area where we live north of Fort Worth, Texas, the city does not offer the usual water and sewage services. To accommodate, all of the homes have aerobic septic systems, which are, for lack of a technical explanation let's just call it a private waste water treatment station. Our septic system processes what our family deposits into the drains, toilets and showers inside our home. In short, we are responsible for our own waste.

One afternoon, my son Tucker, flushed the toilet in the bathroom near the family room. When he pushed the lever, it began making strange gurgling and belching sounds. Although only nine years old, he intuitively knew this sure wasn't a good sign.

"Daddy, come quick!" Tucker yelled. "The toilet is talking to me!"

As my wife Leslie and I made our way to the other side of the house, we were met by an invisible wall of stench. When I say "wall," I mean a wall of odor that we felt when we ran into it. Our eyes began to water, and our lungs were reduced to short shallow breaths. Gagging and coughing, we trudged ahead. The smell was horrific. It wouldn't have surprised me to have seen the paint sliding down the sheetrock.

Leslie was the first to fight through the bitter fog and into the war zone, formerly known as the bathroom. Her scream confirmed my suspicion – the sewage lines to our septic tanks had backed up. Raw sewage was backing up into our sinks, toilets and showers. We had "stuff" coming out of every plumbing fixture on that end of the house.

My beautiful home that usually smelled like a combination of my wife's perfume, laundry detergent and last night's dinner, now smelled like the working end of a waste treatment plant. I began to open the doors and windows to help eliminate the smell. I walked out on my front porch to find that not only had stinky, raw sewage taken over the aroma of our house, but it dominated our neighborhood as well. Our poor neighbors had to smell it too. Our house had "blessed" the entire neighborhood with a house warming present that we have nicknamed the funk!

Are you getting a whiff of this?

We called a plumber, and thankfully he came out that afternoon. After he diagnosed and fixed our gastric backup, I asked him what caused the blockage. His answer was simple and to the point – our family had flushed "non-deteriorating items" into the pipes that blocked the normal flow. While we had a 500-gallon septic tank, the non-deteriorating items had clogged the entire system.

"If there's one thing in life you don't want to backwash on you," he commented on his way out the door, "it's a septic line."

As I waved him goodbye, I mumbled under my breath, "Information I could have used when I bought this place in the country!"

For the next few days, Leslie hovered around the house dressed like a space woman. With a backpack sprayer filled with a strong mixture of bleach and water, she attacked every contaminated area, attempting to kill the germs and eliminate the dominating smell of sewage in our house.

If I ever doubted that my nose had a memory, the matter has been
settled. I can still get a whiff of our cesspool to this day. (I just
had a shiver run through my body as I re-lived that smell. Yuck!)

Marc

WHAT'S IN YOUR PIPES?

Have you ever met someone who has the odor of a backed up septic
system? We are not talking about bad body odor. No, this is far
more distinct. This aroma comes from the rotten matter flushed
into their heart that was never intended to be there.

No matter the age of the item, these things appear to be non-
deteriorating. They are ageless. They never seem to go away. It's
an odor being emitted from their hearts of the flushed things that
were never intended to be deposited there. These things always
haveway of coming back up.

Our hearts do not perform well when we flush non-deteriorating
items into them. Because they were not designed to hold or process
such things, the heart will inevitably spit it back up. Just like the
human body rids itself of toxins, the heart does the same. Given
enough time, stress and opportunity, our words and thoughts will
always indict us.

As you have already learned, we are very different. This area of
our hearts and our words is no different. David doesn't say what
is on his mind until he first processes his thoughts over and over.
You need to ask David what he is thinking. He appears hesitant
with his words, but he's just cautious. He wants to make sure that
the words he uses are exact and accurate to explain what he is trying
to communicate. David's mind often overrides his heart. He looks
like he is easy-going and calm, but he is not at all. Like a duck on
a pond, everything on the surface looks calm and serene, but under

the water, he is paddling his legs off. He is constantly processing, learning and connecting.

On the other hand, you always know what Marc is thinking. Just listen. His mouth is directly connected to his heart. You don't have to ask him what he is thinking. It comes out on its own. Marc tends to talk while he is thinking. He is constantly creating images and words that describe the moment in which he is living. Marc speaks in color. In many ways, he is much more easily understood than David, because he instinctively speaks what is in his heart. His heart can, at times, override his mind. Marc tends to think it is easier to ask forgiveness than permission with his words. He talks. He can't help it.

No matter what our personalities, the fact remains that what is in the heart ultimately comes out in our lives. When Solomon described the hard-wiring of men and women, he observed: *"For as he thinks in his heart, so is he"* (Proverbs 23:7 NKJV). Jesus said it this way, *". . . out of the overflow of the heart the mouth speaks"* (Matthew 12:34 NIV). Oftentimes, the overflow of the heart to our mouths or minds seems to be the backwash of a nasty cesspool. Jesus wasn't making a really good philosophical statement. He was stating a principle that is as certain as gravity itself.

Before the day of the sewer back-up, the Owings family had flushed the toilet countless times without any issues. But it just took one time for everything to back up. We are not sure what or who clogged the sewer lines, but when it all came up, we didn't just see the one "non-deteriorating" . . . everything in the septic tank moved in for a visit!

Tucker was the unfortunate one in their family. All he did was push the lever, and the entire family's waste backed up on him!

He had pushed that lever a thousand times. It had always worked perfectly. Everything in that toilet went exactly where it was supposed to go. This time it backed up on him. Sadly, most of the time, it is those closest to us who stand at the open end of our cesspools. Our "stuff" gets on them.

What we have to share in the remainder of this chapter is not just for your benefit, but it is for your spouse and children as well. Don't move forward without engaging your heart and mind. This is a time to focus and be honest . . . both for your own heart as well as for the health of your relationships.

So we ask you: What has been flushed into your heart? Is it jealousy, fear, competition, abandonment, rage, anger, depression, greed, hurt, unforgiveness, performance or addictions? Whatever poison you picked, whatever junk was passed to you from past generations, the results are the same: What goes in WILL come out. Sooner or later, everything comes up. What's in your pipes?

If you were abandoned, then the backwash of abandonment will come up. If anger is in your heart, anger will be regurgitated in your life. If pride, then pride. If fear, then fear. If perfectionism, then demanding perfection. If abuse, then . . . you get the picture. Whatever ends up in your heart will bubble up in your life.

That is why there is an all-out war for your heart. Whether you realize it or not, whether you acknowledge it or not, there is a war on. And your heart is the most valued ground. If the war is for the heart, then the battle is for the mind. You see, the mind is the gateway to the heart, and the heart is the control console of your actions. So what flows into your mind ultimately dictates ALL of the significant issues of the heart. It sounds like Ol' Solomon was right on.

INCOMING

World War I was a war known for its use of the most advanced military weapons in its time – automatic weapons, aircraft support and multiple transportation options for moving supplies, troops and information. One of the greatest advances in the art of war was displayed in the ability to launch airborne attacks against the enemy. For the first time in the history of wars, missiles and bombs were launched and dropped through the air at supersonic speeds with astounding accuracy and enormous devastation. Because of the speed, altitude and power of these kinds of attack, World War I sounded like no war had ever sounded.

The troops in World War I became all too familiar with the whistling and whirring sound of the different projectiles fired at them. There is a distinct difference in the sound of a bomb exploding in the distance and a missile launched directly at you. Seasoned soldiers knew the difference. They had to. It was a survival skill.

In the heat of battle, one word was used to bring troops to full alert of the life and death reality of an imminent attack: "INCOMING!!!" When someone shouted that warning, troops immediately passed it along and headed for cover. After the explosion, the embattled soldiers instinctively assessed the damage to their own bodies and then began the search for the other men and women in their company.

Joyce Meyer penned an incredible book several years ago entitled *The Battlefield of the Mind*. In her book, she describes Satan's well-developed strategy, custom-made for each of us. Yes, our enemy has devised a battle plan tailored especially for you. His steady stream of suggestions, thoughts and images are relentless in their attack on your mind. Strangely enough, most of us never even notice.

Joyce writes:

"He (Satan) begins by bombarding our mind with cleverly devised patterns of little nagging thoughts, suspicions, doubts, fears, wonderings, reasonings and theories. He moves slowly and cautiously (after all, well-laid plans take time). Remember he has a strategy for his warfare. He has studied us for a long time."

Re-read that quote and feel the weight of Joyce's last sentence: "He has studied us for a long time." You don't have to be a four-star general to understand the significance of this fact. Your enemy has been studying you longer than you know.

The book of Job records an eerie and vivid picture of what Joyce describes in her book.

> *"One day the members of the heavenly court came to present themselves before the LORD, and the Accuser, Satan, came with them. 'Where have you come from?' the LORD asked Satan. Satan answered the LORD, 'I have been patrolling the earth, watching everything that's going on.'"* *(Job 1:6-7 NLT)*

The enemy has been watching us for a long time. He understands our weaknesses, and he is patiently waiting for the most opportune time to deliver his fiery missiles with the most devastation to our hearts. Just like real bombs are purposefully designed to wound, damage, destroy and kill as many people as possible, the devil's weapons against us are meant to inflict maximum damage and death to us and our dear ones. Ultimately, he is trying to kill our hearts.

We have a patient enemy. He doesn't go for the knock out punch every day. Instead, he slowly de-sensitizes us, so that we will eventually accept his destruction as if it were a gift from God Himself. The goal is slow dismantling of boundaries, norms and moral absolutes. His main tool in wearing us down is through that which is most familiar to us – our culture. It is the stuff we see every day.

We live in a society of suggestions. Woven carefully into almost everything we see, these suggestions constantly bombard our minds, attacking us in ways we may not even be aware of. Billboards, media outlets, primetime television and sporting events are just a few of the high places from which the assaults are being launched. The target . . . the Original Sanctuary. If he kills the heart, he wins the war.

THE BATTLEFRONT

For decades, our culture has been reshaping, redefining and re-presenting concepts of truth, morality and decency. Blatant sexuality, the overemphasis on appearance and the false concepts of happiness are all being skewed and presented as if they were *real*. There is a full frontal assault to convince us that sexual immorality is normal, rabid consumerism can buy a more fulfilling life and happiness comes from looking a certain way.

Do you see what is happening, or are you already numb to its effects? What we have bought into and come to think of as acceptable is rotting our minds and killing our souls. We have been under siege so long that we no longer recognize the war. The despicable has become daily normalcy. We have become so tolerant that the boundaries of morality are unrecognizable. It doesn't take long for the lines to become very blurry. What one generation tolerates, the next generation will embrace. And this generation has its hands full.

Make no mistake, there is a lot at stake in this war. The battle-ground is for our beliefs, ideals and perceptions. As the moment-by-moment barrage of explosions detonate in our minds, we slowly lose our moral compass and a clear view of absolutes. Our point of reference becomes the culture instead of the Word of God.

Look around, everything seems to be knocking at the door of your mind. Why? Because the enemy knows that the mind is the gateway to your heart. In a society so consumed with what we put into our bodies ("You are what you eat"), it is a shame that we do not concern ourselves with what we put in our minds. The war is for the heart, and the battlefield is the mind. What you think could be killing you.

"Incoming!" The battle is on. You are in it, whether you realize it or not. Get your head down! You are in a fox hole, and bullets are flying . . .

FIRST LINE OF DEFENSE

Satan knows how to reason like a man. He has been watching us for such a long time that he sees the way our minds work. Like a cunning hunter, he baits the trap and lures us in for a slow kill. How can we go about guarding our minds and avoiding his trap? Since his first line of attack is aimed at our minds, this is where our first line of defense must be set.

Thoughts are like seeds planted in the ground, which prove over time to be either weeds or fruitful crops. Whether good or bad, every seed pops up where it's planted. In this way, modern psychology tells us that thoughts are like seeds. Thus, a bad thought ultimately results in bad behavior. Good thoughts result in good stuff. Seeds always reproduce after themselves.

The pattern goes like this: A *thought* becomes a *belief.* The *belief* becomes a *feeling.* The *feeling* becomes an *action.* The *action,* over time, becomes an *ingrained behavior.*

THOUGHT
    BELIEF
        FEELING
            ACTION
                INGRAINED BEHAVIOR

Let's use a personal example to help us understand how this works.

Tom's marriage is not great. Well, that is actually a huge understatement. He and his wife are not connected at any level. They are more like roommates than husband and wife. For some time, Tom has had little hope of his marriage ever getting any better. He is cynical, uninterested and disconnected.

One day at the office, Tom started sharing with his co-worker, Susan, about the present climate in his household. In a fit of honesty, he told her everything he wished he could tell his wife, but couldn't. Susan was well-meaning and listened intently to all that Tom had to say. After months of the cold shoulder at home, Tom was finally getting some much-needed attention.

Tom's new-found "counselor" thoughtfully suggests that, "Maybe you just married the wrong person. God wants you to be happy, doesn't He?"

After a few more pleasantries, the conversation was over. Tom walked away a little stunned that he just unpacked so much of his emotional luggage with Susan, a practical stranger. "Why did I just do that?" he asked himself. *(Answer: Out of the mouth, the heart speaks.)*

Shaking his head and getting back to work, Tom chalked it up as a harmless conversation. Susan was nice and caring, and he really appreciated her response to his situation, but it was no big deal, right? Right. It was just a thought.

On the drive home that afternoon, Tom thought again about Susan and their encounter in the break room. He replayed the conversation in his mind . . .

DANGER! BELLS! WHISTLES! SIRENS! ALARMS! MAYDAY!!!!!

What? Aren't we overreacting a bit? After all, he's just thinking, right? Precisely the point: he is thinking. What *was* just a thought in the afternoon came back and became the thought that is occupying his mind. Mayday! We have seed on the ground, and it is growing!

Unchecked, this thought will take on a life of its own. The power of a thought and its ability will take Tom, and you, much further than either of you ever intended to go.

The danger of Tom's thought was not in the initial conversation. No, its real power was unleashed when he replayed it in his mind. Unless we acknowledge our thoughts, see them for what they really are, we won't get rid of them before they do their damage.

Truth: Tom is thinking a thought that is a lie. He is thinking on something that is toxic and fatal.

In the heat of an assault, there is not time to process or manipulate a thought into something that is safe to be in your mind. If it is a lie, it has to be thrown out quickly. In Tom's situation, he did not have the emotional intelligence to see the attack coming, much less fight against it. Hurting and wounded people are not strong enough to slosh around in an emotionally-charged situation and respond with integrity. Tom's only defense is to get rid of the poisonous thoughts immediately.

Exactly what lies was he toying with? One – God is consumed with his personal happiness. The other – he is married to the wrong person. Both of these are not true. They are lies. First, God never says that He is all about our happiness. Second, God is sovereign over all things, and he hates divorce. Therefore, Tom couldn't possibly have married the wrong person.

Remember the progression of thought that we outlined earlier. It's not just a thought . . . it is the start of something destructive. Unless Tom recognizes the danger of his thoughts, they will take on a life of their own.

According to our Progression of Thought Model, where could Tom's situation end up?

Thought: "Susan is really attractive. Maybe I did marry the wrong person. God *does* want me to be happy, doesn't He?"

Belief: "I did marry the wrong person. And yes, God does want me to be happy."

Feeling: "I really like the fact that Susan took time to listen to me and gave me some well-deserved sympathy. It feels really good for her to care. If I feel it, it must be right."

Action: The next day, Tom talks to Susan again. She responds with more sympathy than before. He disconnects even more from his wife and begins connecting with his new friend. A new relationship begins.

Ingrained Behavior: It's all down hill from there . . .

What began as "just" a thought could be the end of a marriage.
The enemy gets at us with "harmless" thoughts. And if we don't
recognize them for the lies they are, they will destroy us.

THE POINT OF NO RETURN

In the progression of a thought – belief – feeling – action – ingrained behavior, please be fully aware that the "feeling" stage
is the most dangerous. Most often, it is the point of no return.
We live in a culture that teaches us, "If it feels good, it must be
true." Good or bad, feelings can outweigh rationale. Feelings
take a thought from the mind to the heart and thus become
powerful catalysts of action. Feelings are like a barbed hook;
when attached to the thought, they are practically impossible
to remove. When the feelings get strong enough, changing
our course is usually not an option.

Strong emotions and feelings almost always override intellect.
When feelings become strong enough, our brains slide to the other
side of the car and our hearts take the wheel. Once this happens,
lies are believed, bad choices are made and lives are affected. As
feelings turn to actions, habits of thought and response are formed
and ingrained patterns are cemented into our lives.

Normal people don't set out to destroy their lives, abandon
their spouses and hurt their kids. No one wakes up on a Tuesday
morning and says, "Hey, I think I'll destroy my family today."
Prisons are filled with drug addicts and murderers, but none of
them set out to be so. Singles' bars are filled with men and women
who disconnected from their loved ones and pushed them away,
without ever realizing the end game result of their decisions
and words.

How does it happen? It all begins with a thought. A lie is believed. The feelings it generates are embraced. The emotion overtakes intellect. Then, there is action . . . lives are ruined.

The mind is the gateway to the heart, and it must be guarded at all costs. If we are ever to reclaim those parts of our hearts that have been lost in the fight, we have to become more self-aware – aware of our weaknesses, wounds, abuses, anger and perfectionist tendencies. You can't become more self-aware by being smarter. This is not done with intellect. You need emotional intelligence. That is, becoming fully alive to what you are feeling and thinking and the relationships that surround you.

Self-awareness is the key. You have to be aware of what you are feeling and thinking. You must increase your emotional intelligence. You have to ask yourself the tough questions. You aren't getting the right answers because you aren't asking the right questions. Learn to confront the hard stuff. The next time you find yourself in an awkward or uncomfortable situation, ask yourself these questions:

Why do I think like this?

Why do I respond that way?

Why do I believe that?

Is this a truth or just a passing feeling?

"Above all else, guard your heart, for it is the wellspring of life." (Proverbs 4:23 NIV)

It is just a thought.

JOURNAL

JOURNAL

CHAPTER 6
The Electric Chair

"AND ABOUT THAT TIME GOD SHOWED UP."
FORREST GUMP

MARC

There are different kinds of kids in this world. Some just seemed to be loaded with athletic ability. You know the ones I am talking about – everything in sports they participate in comes so dog-gone easy to them, which makes the rest of us feel . . . well, average.

Then there are the good kids. These kids might be eight years old, but they seem to have the wisdom and conscience of a forty-year-old. Their life-compass always seems to point toward doing the right thing at the right time.

Then there are kids who reflect my childhood. Free spirits! My kind don't think before we speak or act. Nope, we just go with the impulses of the heart. Whatever comes natural is always what comes out. These kids are scary. They look like ordinary kids, but don't be mistaken by the baby-faced countenance . . . they are not ordinary at all. They have the body and emotional maturity of a child but the knowledge of an adult. By the way, this is a lethal combination.

My first encounter with pornography happened when I was just five years old. For the next seven years, I continued to look and be curious. I became all too accustomed to the images. I saw them so often, I grew numb to their power and sway over my life. Grown-up perversion trapped inside of a little boy is a frightening and saddening thought. I was an elementary school student with a graduate level addiction. Sadly, as I got older it actually got worse.

At age twelve, I gave up my virginity, and from that point on, the pornography found in magazines or movies was not an issue. I didn't need it any longer. I had discovered the real thing.

Sexual promiscuity and its unchecked expression was the powerful drug that had my heart spellbound and temporarily comforted. The thoughts and images from my earlier childhood had been replaced by an actual feeling. This feeling seemed to medicate my wounds and emptiness. The antidote to the black hole of validation that lay at the center of my being was being temporarily filled by my physical and emotional addiction to sex.

The addiction fooled me into thinking that I was in control of my life and my feelings that I had some kind of free pass to do what I wanted when I wanted to do it. But instead of moving me toward some sense of normalcy, my new "medication" threw me off a cliff. The addiction lied.

Lust filled my thoughts, emotions and creative energy. Like a fire that could not be put out, it demanded fuel to insure its survival. To say that it consumed me would be an understatement. All the images and experiences of my past that were imbedded in my mind tormented me every minute of the day. I never had to buy another magazine or rent a video because my mind had an embedded reel of movie-quality footage of perversion. It was accessible to me at any moment.

Addiction is a dominating and relentless opponent. The more you give, the more it takes. It cannot be satisfied. You begin by consuming it. Ultimately, it consumes you. The hunter becomes the hunted.

By the time I was 19, I had been ridden hard and put up wet! I was tired, fatherless, lonely, angry and most of all, broken. The thought of living to my 21st birthday was unfathomable. What was left of my heart was severely damaged from years of self abuse, drug abuse and every other kind of abuse you can think of.

Broken and lifeless, I staggered into a church service at the Bethel Temple Church in Fort Worth, Texas. I had nowhere else to go. I had nowhere else to turn. Maybe God could or would help me. I was desperate. I went to church, walked in and grabbed a seat in the back row.

An unknown preacher stood behind a pulpit and shared a stirring message that shook me to the core of who I was. God spoke through this man, directly to me. He talked about Jesus love for me. He told me how Jesus had died on the cross for MY sin. I somehow understood what he was saying to me. My heart felt something real and tangible for the first time in years.

In the middle of this preacher's message, he just stopped. He looked into the audience and said that the Lord had given him a word of knowledge. And he delivered the Word:

> *"There is a young man here tonight in search of something that he is not even sure exists – a loving God. Young man, you have used alcohol and drugs to mask the pain, but tonight I want to draw you to God. I am calling you out, son, to come and sit in the seat you have longed for all of your life. It is a place where it is not only safe to be you, it's required. It is a place that will shower you completely with the cleansing waters of mercy and love. I am calling you to come to the lap of your heavenly Father."*

That night, I walked alone down the long aisle. At the altar of that church, I met Jesus for the first time in my life. It really was true! I found out that Jesus Christ did exist and He did forgive sins. I knew beyond a shadow of any doubt that God loved me and that I was eternally forgiven from my past.

My life was completely lost until God found me in that church service. I didn't see white lights or get knocked off my feet by the power of God. No, it was much more dramatic than that. I was completely forgiven of my past and released into my future. My heart was healed from the inside out. For the first time, I had a conscience that guided me with truth. For the first time, I had hope. For the first time, I began to dream of a future.

MOVING ON

With my life started and moving in a positive direction, I began to chase my dreams of having a family, being a dad and having a career in the ministry. Jesus freely gave me the graceful gift of forgiveness, but my freedom was much farther down the road. I would have to fight for it.

I met and married Leslie, the girl of my dreams. She has blonde hair and blue eyes and is absolutely the most pure person I have ever met. In fact, it was her purity that first captured my heart and love. She was my opposite in every sense of the word: She was a virgin, she was pure, graduated college, her mom and dad were still happily married and living what I thought was the picture-perfect life on a golf course. Leslie had committed herself to waiting for the Lord to bring the man that she was to marry. As unlikely as this may sound, I was the one she had prayed for.

I don't think I was who she expected to marry, but there was no doubt in her mind that God had chosen me to be her husband. Unlike most couples, Leslie and I started out as true friends. Because we started as friends, I got to be honest about every bad thing I had ever done in my life. I mean it . . . I held nothing back – the good, the bad and the ugly. And even after I told her everything, she did not run away or reject me.

Leslie's limitless compassion and unconditional love for me was the oil of healing that God used to soften the hardened and hurt places of my heart. I remember telling her about that spark of pornography that had started in my heart as a young boy. I attempted to explain how it had exploded into a full on wild fire of unquenchable passion as I got older. No matter how much I tried to get the flames under control, they seemed to ignite other dry places of my heart. The fire was consuming me. Over and over, Leslie expressed the same message, "Honey, God is going to free you!"

A talon-like claw constantly penetrated my mind. Lust gripped me. From the moment I got up until the time I went to bed, my thoughts tormented me. It was a daily encounter with a terminal disease. I do not ever remember, even as a child, having innocent thoughts. Lust had always been in my life. I had never met a woman about whom I did not entertain some form of perverted thoughts. In some shape or form, my mind always went the same direction. It was like the lust had worn a groove in my brain. The perversion of my memories and the feelings of total bondage chiseled away at my heart. I was saved, yet I still felt completely trapped and helpless.

Leslie never judged me. She truly decided to love me in sickness and in health. And I was clearly sick! As defeated as I felt, Leslie never let up with her steady stream of hope for me. She continually encouraged me with the message and hope of God's freedom, but I never believed her.

I learned behavior management skills so I could survive. But I believed in my heart that freedom was not an achievable reality for me. In fact, I remember asking every man I knew if they had ever met someone who was truly free from lust, and every one of them answered the same way: "No, not really." I was not encouraged.

I began my career at James Robison Evangelistic Association on November 15, 1992. My first job was as a Project Coordinator in the Ministry Relations Department. I reported directly to the vice president, Terry Redmon, James' son-in-law. Terry offered a spiritual covering and love that absolutely gave me a chance to reach some of the dreams that were alive in my heart.

Life was moving ahead for me, and I was accomplishing the two basic dreams of my heart: marrying someone I truly loved and being mentored by amazing men in ministry. Even with my dreams coming true, the fire of lust continued robbing my marriage of intimacy and left me feeling like a leper at a dermatologist convention.

The first time I met James Robison, I liked him. When I heard him preach, I believed him. He was everything that I hoped to become. Over my years at the ministry, we became close friends. On one occasion, I remember reluctantly sharing my struggles with him and then bracing up for what I thought he was going to say to me. However, he did not shame me or load me down with more do's and don'ts. James gave me mercy and not justice.

"Marc," he said, "I remember having those same struggles you are fighting, to the point that I wanted to die." Shocked, I couldn't believe his transparency and honesty. Hope filled my heart as he told me how he found freedom. An uneducated carpet cleaner had prayed for him, and he was flooded with release and freedom like he had never known. "Marc, I am completely free from the bondage of lust that used to keep my mind in a demonic vice grip."

James prayed for me that day and asked God to bring the same freedom to my life in His timing. He prayed for a divine appointment.

On August 10, 1994, my divine appointment showed up.

Part of my job description was to pick up guests from the airport who would be appearing on James' television show, LIFE TODAY. This day I was to pick up James Ryle. After getting Mr. Ryle from the DFW Airport, I took him to meet a group of men for a round of golf. As I dropped him off, I told him that I would pick him up later that afternoon and how I was looking forward to hearing him speak.

As I headed back to the office, I soon encountered my worst nightmare. There she stood on the side of the road, waving her hands in what appeared to be a state of emergency. She looked to be about 25 years old and was dressed like she belonged in one of the upscale neighborhoods I was driving near. Her long, dark hair flowed from a straw sun hat that shielded her soft brown eyes, and a Gucci purse draped over her left arm. Her Brazilian accent broke the silence as she explained that her car had stalled and she needed a ride to the gas station.

My mind quickly said yes, wanting to help this woman in distress, but as my mouth said yes, my stomach began to tighten, warning me that I was being led down the wrong path. My spirit was on full alert. Ignoring the alarms in my spirit and dismissing the paranoia, I welcomed her into my car. This proved to be a big mistake.

As soon as we pulled away from the curb, the seduction began. This was no innocent lady stranded on the side of the road, but a woman who knew how to entrap the wealthy men that traveled this road. With every tempting word that flowed from her lips, I felt myself being pulled down into my worst fear . . . but I was defenseless. I was sliding down a slippery slope with no traction to be found. Silently, I prayed, "God help me."

The voice that whispered to me next was familiar, but not holy. "Marc, take her to a hotel, and put it on your credit card. Tell your wife that you bought it for a down-and-out homeless person. She will believe you!" Beyond a shadow of a doubt, I knew that I was about to make the biggest mistake of my life if I agreed with this wicked voice. Even though I clearly knew the right thing to do, I didn't feel like I was in control. I wanted to say no, but all I could do was drive in silence with tears running down my face. I remember her deceiving voice, "Don't cry sweetheart. I will make everything better."

Then it happened.

I pulled over on the side of the road, my heart beating out of my chest, and something took control of my mouth. Tearfully . . . no sobbingly . . . I told her, "Lady, I love my wife, and I can't do this to her."

Enraged, she climbed out of my truck and slammed the door. I sped away as if my life depended on it.

Before you start cheering, I must warn you. This is where things got really interesting. The unholy voice was back, but this time it was quoting scriptures to me. Scriptures that I had never even memorized: "Doesn't the Word say that if a man lusts in his heart, he is guilty as if he had actually committed adultery? How can rusty water and fresh water flow from the same faucet? If a man has sin and claims to walk with God, he only deceives himself." Twisted scripture after twisted scripture bombarded my mind. With each quotation, I felt a wave of unfounded guilt overtaking me.

"Marc, did you want to sleep with her?" it accused.

"Yes, but I didn't."

"That doesn't matter. You thought about it, and truth be told, you are still thinking about it." I looked down at my speedometer, and I was flying down the road at 110 miles an hour.

"Marc, do your wife a favor and end you life," the voice suggested. "Drive this truck into the next bridge. You are not a Christian. You just used Christianity to try to avoid what is coming next, total failure. You will never change."

"God, please help me!" I cried inside. "Please forgive me!"

I was burning from the inside out as I pulled into the driveway at our home. The lady's voice and her words of invitation played over and over in my mind. I wanted to go back. I wanted to give in and do what had been so natural all my life. Old memories and pictures targeted the screen of my mind like fiery missiles. This onslaught of images, voices and guilt made me feel like I would literally lose my mind.

I called my wife at work. I talked and began to weep. "Honey, I am so sorry that you married me." In as much detail as I could get out, I explained what had just occurred. Leslie kept encouraging me and shouting, "Marc you didn't do anything wrong! These are not your thoughts, honey, just hang on, and God will deliver you." I yelled into the phone, "Leslie you were a fool for marrying a guy like me. I will never change and these voices will never go away. This is just who I am, perverted and sick." That was the last thing I said before I hung up the phone.

I wanted to die. I wanted God to take me away from all the pain that I was feeling. The voice in my head had convinced me that I would soon lose my family and my career in one fatal swoop.

That night, I got to the LIFE TODAY *studios early to set up for the television taping. When the taping started, I sat in the very back row, as far away from James Ryle as I could get. I can't remember much of what he said that night, but I do remember the wicked voice accusing me throughout his entire sermon:*

"Marc, if these people knew your thoughts and desires toward women, you would be kicked out of the ministry and fired from this job today. You are a fake! You are sick! You will never change! Tonight, James Ryle will get a word of knowledge, and you will be exposed for who you truly are . . . a sick man."

Toward the end of the service, James began to call people out of the crowd and encourage them with what God had shown him. I was scared to death. Desperately, I tried to hide behind the person in front of me and hoped that he would not make eye contact with me. I slid down in my seat.

Then James Ryle looked my direction and called out my name. "Marc, I have a word from the Lord for you." My seat suddenly felt like an electric chair wired to fry me to a puddle of nothing. Here it came. James was about to dish out exactly what I deserved – judgment.

"Marc," James said, "God showed me that wisdom tested you today. Wisdom tested you today, and you did not do what you thought you would do. Now wisdom is going to court you like lust courted you all of your days. The Spirit of God is now on you, and you will begin to communicate to men and women like you have

spoken to trees." (James Ryle did not know that I had practiced preaching in the woods to the trees that surrounded a pond. I had preached alone, but God had been watching and wanted me to know He had seen me.)

As James spoke, I felt God pull my spirit to Himself. My insides connected to God. I went into my Sanctuary. I was aware that I was still in the studio, but was more keenly aware that I was not. I felt like I was in heaven. In actuality, heaven invaded me. I knew that Jesus was there with me, and I could hear His voice: "Marc, I love you, and everything is going to be better."

"No, no Lord. I don't want to go back," I pleaded. "I cannot live like this anymore."

"I know, son, but everything is going to be different." I opened my eyes as James was finishing what he was saying. While Jesus was speaking to my spirit, James was also speaking. (I had to go back later and listen to the tape to find out everything James had said because I was so consumed by the presence of Jesus.)

When it was all over, I wanted to shout. For the first time in my life, I felt completely clean. Up until that time, I had never had an innocent moment in my thoughts. But when Jesus told me that everything would change, it did. All the thoughts and accusations were gone. My mind and my spirit were clear. I slowly scanned the room, looking at the women, and I did not have one single perverted or lustful thought. Finally, I was free! Jesus had set me free!

I left the studio feeling like I had lost 100 pounds. I was light, and I was free. I drove home singing, praising and laughing. I was practically dancing inside my truck.

When I walked into our house I met Leslie in the hallway. With tears running down my cheeks and a huge smile spreading across my face, I said, "Honey, it's gone. It's really gone. I am free! I am free!"

Leslie fell to her knees, threw her hands toward heaven and exclaimed, "I knew You would set him free! God, thank You for Your faithfulness. I knew You would do it!"

That night was a new beginning for us. I climbed in bed with my wife, and for the first time there was no shame or haunting memories. It was silent. We were finally alone. I was free!

JOURNAL

JOURNAL

CHAPTER 6 1/2
Pull Up A Chair

"NO MAN FOR ANY CONSIDERABLE PERIOD,
CAN WEAR ONE FACE TO HIMSELF, AND
ANOTHER TO THE MULTITUDES, WITHOUT
FINALLY GETTING BEWILDERED AS TO
WHICH MAY BE TRUE."
NATHANIEL HAWTHORNE

DAVID

*In April of 2002, I went on a trip to Ruidoso, New Mexico
with twelve other men. Driving from Fort Worth, Texas in a
fifteen-passenger van with a box trailer in tow for nine and a half
hours, in tight quarters, knee-to-knee, sweatshirt-to-sweatshirt,
brother to brother. Why such a road trip? We were hungry, tired
and bored – hungry for something more than what we had, tired of
things being the same, and bored, quite honestly, with our personal
lives, church lives and God lives. Setting out for a five-day quest,
we were expectant and hopeful . . . but clueless about what lay
ahead for us.*

*Three days deep into the trip, we had a day of fasting from food
and sound. For eight hours, we roamed individually around the
Lincoln National Forest to meet with God. Mid-afternoon of that
day in the wilderness, I was sitting on a fallen tree in a forest of
ponderosa pines at about 9,000 feet above sea level. While I was
sitting there God showed up.*

*And when He did, He came with full force and purpose. He
came after me – uncovering and exposing some of the darkest,
most sinful and embarrassing things of my life. It was the kind of
deep stuff that would make you cringe if it were to run on a big
screen television at your friend's house.*

*For about 45 minutes, an unceasing stream of pictures, words and
vivid memories flooded my mind. Most of what God brought back
to my heart and head was from almost ten years earlier. In this
fast-paced world, 45 minutes might not seem like much time, but it
was long enough to forever alter my life, heart and ministry.*

*In that encounter, the holiness and righteousness of God
unmasked my sins (past and present); indiscretions, resentment,
unmet expectations, unforgiveness, bitterness, anger and malice
poured out like water. Tears flowed as the discipline of my
heavenly Father gave me a strong, steady whiff of my inner
cesspool. My sin was tangible . . . it had a distinct smell to it.
It was real. It was alive. It was definitely mine.*

*I saw my "stuff" like Father sees it. In His grace and mercy, He
grabbed me by the back of the head and forced me to stare at my
own depravity. What I saw staggered me.*

*In the eyes of my Father, I was a liar. I was a cheater. I was a
religious poser. I was immoral and unclean. I was an emotional
adulterer who had emotionally abandoned my wife and given my
heart to a dream of business success and wealth. I was handcuffed
by unforgiveness and chained by bitterness. Integrity and character were almost non-existent.*

*He showed me a picture of my life. I saw five large boxes. On
the side of each box, in my handwriting were these words: Box #1
– **Family**, Box #2 – **Church**, Box #3 – **Business**, Box #4 – **Public**
and Box #5 – **Private**.*

*When I saw the boxes, I knew what the picture meant. My life
was divided into non-integrated parts. The boxes separated each
area from the others. There was no integrity, so I had to hide
in different boxes, different lives. The relationship, actions and
integrity of one box were never seen by any relationship of any of
the others. I had segmented my life to protect myself, to protect the
pretender that was in me from being found out. I heard the voice*

*of God speak to my heart. "David, You don't have a business life, family life, church life, public life and private life. You don't have different lives. You just have a life. It is all **one** life."*

He dumped out my boxes, and my stuff went everywhere.

The first chapter of the Book of James came to my mind: "A double minded man is unstable in all his ways." I thought to myself, "Double-minded? You've have to be kidding! I wish I were only double minded."

I began to confess and agree with everything that He brought up. By name, each instance, I agreed with Him about what I was, who I had become and what my sin was. And then I repented. And repented. And repented. I began to weep uncontrollably.

Strangely enough the sorrow-filled sounds of my repentance began to change. The tearful and breathless encounter with my sin slowly and steadily morphed into praise. As I was released from the grip of God's justice and righteousness, I found myself swimming in His mercy and grace. And all I could do was worship.

It was a purer and more oblivious worship than I had ever experienced. Nothing before had ever compared to this encounter with my King. Complete abandon came over me as I found myself standing atop a large granite boulder 100 times my size. With arms outstretched, head back and voice raised in utter adoration of my God I stood.

From what sounded like a great distance, the mountain wind began to blow. It whistled as it came through the aspens and pines. When I heard it coming, I knew it would blow on me. As I stood on that God-made altar, the winds hit me, first from one direction and then almost simultaneously from the other. It blew and I swayed, back and forth, moving with it as it moved with me. The wind held me as I stood and worshipped my Forgiver, my Healer, my Confronter and my Father. It felt as if I stood there for hours.

The freedom of that moment was like nothing I had ever experienced before. Freedom was tangible. It too had a taste, but much, much sweeter than my sin that so staggered me only moments earlier. The truth of His Word became a reality in my heart. "It is for freedom that Christ has set us free"(Galatians 5:1 NIV).

As the emotion and the reality of this encounter began to subside, it dawned on me that something was radically different inside of me. I was clean. I was burden-less. And I was forgiven. I walked out of that forest upright, free, hope-filled and whole.

Because we each spent the day of fasting in total silence, I told no one what had happened to me. I privately enjoyed the forgiveness of my Father and enjoyed the silence, not having to engage anyone else. My forgiveness was sweet. It was real, and it was mine! I went to bed that night more free than I had been in a long time.

After breakfast on Sunday morning, the group settled in for a day of teaching and reflection on what God had begun in us. Many of the men shared what Father had shown, spoken and done with them during our day in the wilderness. I just kept quiet.

I was scheduled to teach that night at 7:00. The thought of speaking to this particular group of warriors intimidated me. What would I say? Would they receive me? Most of these guys are smarter than I am!

About 4:00 that afternoon, I made my way back to my house to think about what I would share with the men. I was looking through the Word, jotting down some thoughts but with very little connectivity, realizing that I had nothing much to say. My mind began to wander, and I prayed, "God, would you give me something decent to say? Help me here. I am supposed to teach tonight."

As I sat at that table, staring at my Bible, the only recurring thought that I had was, "Tell them your story." Every time it popped up my mind, I pushed it back down like a burp after a slice of pepperoni pizza. "I can't tell my story. I'll be exposed. I wouldn't be the nice guy who can teach anymore. It's not really my story to tell anyway. It is our story (mine and April's). Godly people don't talk about this kind of stuff. God, this can't be you."

Instead of doing the obedient thing and agreeing with the Holy Spirit, I wrote down some unconnected thoughts and decided to make up the rest.

At 6:55 on that beautiful Sunday evening, I walked back across the street to the house where I was to teach. As the others gathered in the large den, I stepped outside onto a deck overlooking the forest. After only a few seconds, I heard the telephone ring inside the house. I heard a voice call out,

"D.T. It's for you. It's April."

I walked in the house and reached for the telephone. "Hello," I said.

"Hi," April responded.

"Are you okay?" I asked, a little concerned.

"Yes. I just felt like I needed to tell you something."

"We are just about to sit down, and I am about to speak. What is it?" I questioned her.

"Well . . ." (long pause), "David, if you are thinking about telling our story, the stuff from a long time ago, I think that these men are supposed to hear it. I release you to tell our story. I know that sounds crazy, but I think it is right."

(Longer pause . . .) "Okay, April. If you think so." I swallowed hard.

"I love you."

"I love you too."

I was numb to the core, like I had received an intravenous dose of Novocain. The room went silent. My heart jumped. My pulse raced, and my spirit did a back flip in my belly. Under my breath I mumbled, "God, You don't fight fair." After a few moments I gathered myself. I looked like I was composed, but I never truly recovered.

As the men gathered in the room, I pulled a chair from the end of dining room table. With the size of the group, it felt awkward to stand while speaking. My recollection of the chair is that it was a straight-backed, wooden, heavy, Spanish-style chair with thick, wide arms. It was very uncomfortable.

*From that seat, I started teaching. After about 20 minutes of
attempting (unsuccessfully) to be brilliant, I gave up. I told a
man in the rear of the room to turn off the recording devices.
For the next five minutes, I told those twelve men things that no
one on the planet knew about me. It felt like forever.*

*Through tears and brokenness, I shared my failures, hurts,
wounds, sin and utter depravity. I told them about my darkest
and deepest flaws and mistakes. I told how Father had met me
on that mountain the day before. I allowed them entrance into
my secret place, turned the lights on in my darkest corners and
letting them smell my inner cesspool.*

*When I finished speaking, there was a long silence. My friend
Richard Henderson broke the silence and said, "I have known you
a long time, and I never knew any of that about you. I am so sorry
that you have lived alone with that all of these years. I am so, so
sorry. David . . . I love you, bro."*

*I awkwardly acknowledged his comment and tried to get out of
the chair. Before I could get up, all the men gathered around
me. They prayed aloud for me . . . very loud. They blessed me,
encouraged me and affirmed me. They blessed my wife and prayed
God's healing and restoration over us. They felt my pain and lifted
my burden. Their heavy, hairy and calloused hands were like a
balm to my soul. When they touched me everything lifted off.
It was the same kind of release I had felt on the mountain, but
different. They told me they loved me and gave me their word
that they would never share my secrets. My name would be safe
in their mouths, forever.*

*I gathered myself, got out of the chair and collapsed on a blue
leather couch in the center of the room. Things got quiet and*

*awkward. As I tried to compose myself I realized something.
Every man in the room was staring at that chair – straight-backed,
wooden and uncomfortable – sitting at the front of the room . . .
and empty.*

We sat there in a tense, yet holy silence. Then it happened.

*Another man got up from his seat and found his way to the chair.
He sat down, squirmed a little and began to talk. He told his story,
revealed his sins and weaknesses. He unpacked baggage of his
life that had been hidden for years. He was scared, but he did it
anyway. And when he was done, he too was accepted, comforted
and prayed over. The same gift that had been extended to me was
granted to him. After he left the chair, another man climbed in.
Then another. Then another.*

*For the next five hours, men took the chair in bondage, guilt,
affliction, addiction and sin. They left the chair renewed and
restored. A man named Keith even found the salvation of God in
that chair. Years of going to church and God found him while he
was sitting in that wonderfully awful chair.*

*While each of our experiences were a little different that night,
we all found the same thing. After years of bondage to guilt,
shame, neglect, sin and abuse, disappointment and unforgiveness –
no matter what the story, we all received the same thing . . .
FREEDOM.*

DIVINE APPOINTMENTS
*Until that day on the mountain and my night in the chair, I
was forgiven of my sin, but I was not free. My confession and
repentance before God brought my forgiveness. My confession
before twelve other men released my freedom.*

Three particular passages of Scripture teach what thirteen men experienced in New Mexico in April, 2002:

"If we confess our sins, He is faithful and just to forgive us our sins and to cleanse us from all unrighteousness." (I John 1:9 NKJV)

"Is any one of you sick? He should call the elders of the church to pray over him and anoint him with oil in the name of the Lord. And the prayer offered in faith will make the sick person well; the Lord will raise him up. If he has sinned, he will be forgiven. Therefore confess your sins to each other and pray for each other so that you may be healed. The prayer of a righteous man is powerful and effective." (James 5:14-16 NIV)

"It is for freedom that Christ has set us free. Stand firm, then, and do not let yourselves be burdened again by a yoke of slavery . . . You, my brothers, were called to be free." (Galatians 5:1, 13 NIV)

After coming down the mountain, I did a word study to get a better understanding of what these scriptures were telling me to do. Because of my business background, what I found was particularly fascinating to me. I discovered that one of the root forms of the word confess was derived from a real estate term defining "ownership," "title" and "authority."

Wow! I finally got it – I have to "own" my stuff. It has to be mine. I can't run from it, pass the buck or deed it to someone else. The truth of this principle requires that I own my sin, pain and sickness. I don't have to be sick. I can choose to not be. The truth is: I am only as sick as my secrets.

No matter what has been embedded in your heart, its removal will require your acknowledgement. Your sin – adultery, affairs, bortion, every form of abuse from and to you, anger, abandonment, ejection, lying, cheating, disappointment, stealing, (fill in the blank) whatever is taking up valuable space in your Sanctuary can be re- oved by applying God's principle.

all a friend. Go see your pastor. Visit with a counselor. Ask them pray for you and over you. Unpack the pain and sign over the ed to your heavenly Father. You don't have to live with this any nger. Ask God and the Holy Spirit to remove it, seal it and redeem Whatever is lodged in your sanctuary will no longer be a life chor, but a life launcher. It is about to become high-octane fuel r the rest of your life.

ow, here's the hard part . . . WAIT. Your healing and freedom may instantaneous. But sometimes it is not. Most times it is not. It is ore of a process. Begin right now praying for a divine appointment. ie frustrating thing about waiting for a divine appointment is the ivine One is setting the schedule. It is His time not yours. On the her hand, the wonderful thing about a divine appointment is it is ways worth the wait. When Divine shows up, nothing is ever e same. Pray and ask God for your time, a time in which your nfession and honesty intersects with his healing touch.

arc's ultimate healing from sexual addiction was seven years after he ve his heart and life to Jesus. My healing from fear and depression curred over three years after I unpacked the pain in my heart with class full of people. Just do your part, and wait for an appointment th your Daddy. He will come . . . we promise.

E REST OF THE STORY

ose 12 other men, well, some of them are now my best friends. All them are my heroes. They went where I had never seen anyone go fore. In those five days on that mountain, we took a leap off the high *board into a life we had only imagined. We discovered that there was more life found in the jumping and the water of God's mercy and grace was deep enough to handle us all. We have never been the same.*

ARE YOU READY FOR A CHANGE?

Opening up may be hard, but don't you think it's worth the risk? Are you sick and tired of being sick and tired? Take the time to climb up into the Sanctuary of your heart. Go back in your memory and open the doors to some of the rooms you haven't entered in a while. Ask your Father to meet you there. Ask the Holy Spirit to go with you. It may look straight-backed, wooden and uncomfortable, but it is a seat of freedom.

Come on . . . pull up a chair.   *David*

JOURNAL

JOURNAL

CHAPTER 7
A Trip To The
Tree House

"TOO MANY PEOPLE, TOO MANY DEMANDS, TOO MUCH TO DO. COMPETENT, BUSY, HURRYING PEOPLE- IT JUST ISN'T LIVING AT ALL." ANN MORROW LINDBERGH

MARC

As I am writing my thoughts for this final chapter, I am in one of my secret places. This place is not mine. I don't own it, and I didn't build it. I have absolutely no earthly equity in it. It was offered by some dear friends. A couple of years ago, they gave me an open-ended invitation to sit on their back porch anytime that I wanted.

This secret place is hidden in the northwest corner of Ft. Worth, Texas. My friend's home sits on a hill with Eagle Mountain Lake as the backdrop. It's cool and breezy in the mornings. Because of its westward view, it produces spectacular sunsets in the evenings. It has become a favorite place to get alone with the Lord. Many hours have been logged just sitting, thinking and spending time with the Lord in this magnificent spot.

Although my friends now are different than in childhood and the sanctuary is located in a different place, the purpose has remained the same. When I come here, God shows up. It is quiet. It is secret. And it is secluded. When I call David and say, "Meet me at the lake," he knows exactly where to go. Our friends' back porch is one of the tree houses where I meet the God of the universe, Abba Daddy.

This book began in a childhood memory of THE tree house. Remember? The big oak tree with the lumber yard nailed to the top of it. That boyhood tree house was my first encounter with a secret place. It was the first time that I remember wanting to go away. I don't ever remember feeling the desire to run away; I just wanted to go away for a while.

*What I now realize, but didn't know then, is the big old tree was
an earthly expression of a heavenly reality. Unknowingly we
created in that tree what we longed for in our hearts – privacy,
safety, comfort and seclusion. We had no idea what we had
created. Nevertheless, it was exactly what we all longed for.
The woods near my home were my secret place, and the tree
house became my sanctuary.*

*Only my closest friends knew where the tree house was hidden.
Every boy who built the tree house had an unspoken equity in it.
They owned part of this creation. If you were speaking to any of
the kids who worked on the old tree all you would have to say was,
"I'll meet you at the tree." Just like clockwork they would be in
the old tree house waiting on me. The map to the sanctuary was
etched into their minds, and the key to the door was simply that
they knew where it was. Their equity guaranteed their acceptance.*

Marc

DAVID

*One of the greatest common denominators of humanity is the
inborn, desperate need for comfort and safety. The human need
for safety begins in the womb and is carried all the days of our
lives. When my son Gibson was born, I received my first lesson
in child development from his attending nurse. After checking his
vitals and changing his diaper, she called to me. "Dad, let me
show you how to wrap up your son." I inched a little closer.*

*I watched her lay out the hospital blanket in a triangle shape under
Gibson's 10 pound, 2 ounce body. When she placed him on the
blanket, he was un-touched and obviously vulnerable. Cold and
exposed, he began to squirm and draw his knees to his chest and
his little fists to his chin. When he curled up, the nurse went into
high gear. She began wrapping him tightly with the blankets in*

the crib. She wrapped and tied him in those blankets like she was a calf-roping contestant at the National Finals Rodeo. When she finished, the only things that he could move were his head and his eyes. She packed him and wrapped him until he was stiff as a board.

"Is that too tight?" I asked. "Is he comfortable?" The nurse responded, "He's just fine. The tighter the better. It makes him feel safe. Almost like he's still in the womb. Now, Dad, hold him close so he can hear your heartbeat."

David

We are hard-wired with a deep, bottomless longing for a place in which we are safe. The deepest places of our souls long for a place of refuge to shelter us from the winds of life. A place where the traffic of our mind is quieted and we once again hear our hearts' desires and longings. We need to be safe. We long to be safe. We must find that place where we are safe.

The deepest parts of our hearts long for Daddy. It longs for a place of protection, acceptance, safety, inclusion and belonging. It longs for the place where we receive identity, where we relate to something and someone bigger, wiser, smarter, more infinite, more loving and eternally certain.

This longing is internal evidence that we were intended to live as children of God. Adults and babies alike need the protection of a tightly-tied blanket around them. For me, as a grown man, to admit it and do something about it . . . that's a whole different question.

My heavenly Father created me with needs. As sure as He made my heart, He also created its contents. Needs are also His creation. He is not a cruel, wild-haired tyrant. He isn't sadistically producing in me a miserable and helpless cycle of emptiness and discomfort. Nope. He has a plan. A divine plan.

He created it so I could and would run to Him. He created a space, a vacuum, a blank spot in my heart and emotions that can only be filled by Him. The place is shaped like His presence. I am made in His image. His finger prints are smeared all over my body, soul and spirit. My need for safety and security can only be met by the Father. I need to hear His heartbeat.

Needs don't make us weak, they make us human. We are not flawed or imperfect because we are needy. We were created with unquenchable thirst in our hearts for things that are not found in this world. We are needy by design. We were created for fulfillment and safety by the Creator. He is the only element that can meet our deepest needs. Sadly, we usually stop far short and settle for much less. In denying and medicating our needs, we choose a half-hearted existence.

We are usually chasing other things. We are feasting on the counterfeit of our culture while the most real reality of the universe waits patiently for our visit. Most people detest the feeling of being needy. It feels weak, vulnerable. For men, it feels un-masculine and child-like. For women, it feels helpless, uncovered or bare. We don't like neediness, so we pretend that we are not.

Some Christians think that it is practically un-godly to be needy or have any desires at all. We are not supposed to need or desire anything. This couldn't be further from the truth. We are NOT too needy. In fact, we aren't needy enough. In actuality, we are far too easily satisfied.

In his book *Desiring God,* John Piper said it this way:

"It is not a bad thing to desire our own good. In fact the great problem of human beings is that they are far too easily pleased. They don't seek pleasure with nearly the resolve and passion that they should. And so they settle for mud pies of appetite instead of the infinite delight (in God)" (*Desiring God* page 17).

While we all need such a place, very few have it. In fact, we would say that most don't. No matter your occupation, race, creed or color: everyone has need for safety and seclusion. We don't want it bad enough. And we don't listen to our hearts. If our ears were tuned to our hearts' desire, we would hear what we need, we would be running to the places where our hearts are filled.

We were designed for a higher place. Although we are living in the world, there is an upward pull on the heart of every human on the planet. Our hearts and souls were branded with an internal compass directing us to another place. We instinctively long for lengthy vision, blissful rest, perfect protection and eternal value. However, vision, rest, protection and eternal value don't exist in any tangible form on this planet. Nevertheless, we long for them. Deeply and quietly, we long for them.

C.S. Lewis once wrote: "If I find myself with a desire which no experience in this world can satisfy, the most probable explanation is that I was made for another world."

We were made for another world. Most of us are unknowingly longing for another world. The frustration is that we are (temporarily) trapped in this one. Humans long for the things of heaven even if they say they don't believe in it. Every human.

No one is exempt. A cowboy, Methodist minister, school teacher, Franciscan monk, drug addict or atheist . . . doesn't really matter what you are or who you are. You have the need for safety and protection. God made you that way whether you acknowledge it or not. The need for value, safety and seclusion covers every human being – every race, creed, religious system, color and nationality. We all long for a place that is safe, secure and secluded. We are looking for the Original Sanctuary.

In chapter 2, we gave you the definition of sanctuary: "sacred place," "a place of giving refuge or asylum," "a private place" and "free of intrusion."1

Where is that place again? The tree house of your heart, with your heavenly Father.

We all need a place to get quiet. We need a place where our spiritual ears are engaged. We need a place where traffic, bills, practices, sermons and soccer games cannot interrupt and distract. We need a place where life is reduced to its simplest and most profound form . . . us and God. We were *hard-wired from the factory* with a need for regular trips to the tree house.

BUSYNESS IS THE ENEMY

High-speed lifestyles crammed with calendars, league schedules, church responsibilities, washing clothes and email are choking our spirits. Our bodies and minds are running at warp speed while our spirits, our hearts are starving for the attention of their Maker. But we just can't seem to stop the madness and the fury of it all. We stay busy, busy, busy on the outside while our insides slowly run down like an unwound clock. Some of you are thinking, "David. Marc. This tree house stuff is for someone else. I can't do this.

I don't have time." If that is what is rattling around in your head, we have one question: How's that working for you?

If your life had a fuel gauge, would you be closer to empty or full? Time away in the sanctuary is the filling station for our hearts!

Authentic relationship cannot be timed or scheduled. It must be fluid and constant. While religion can be programmed and scheduled, authentic relationships must be dynamic. This relationship between you and the Creator is a daily, constantly-changing thing. It takes on a life of its own. It must be constant and steady. It must be friendly, warm, engaging and real.

THE NEW ADDICTION

If we are to ever get to the center of our hearts, the busyness must stop, at least for a while. Busyness is the enemy of any significant time spent in the tree house. We are too busy to stop, listen and hear the heart of our Father: "Come away with me my child."

God's call is continuous, never ceasing. He is calling us to friendship and companionship. But our busyness keeps us away from the greatest friendship possible.

Our nation is running rampant with addictions. The use of sex, drugs and alcohol are at frightening and alarming levels. The age groups that are affected are becoming younger and younger in our society. Elementary age kids are now doing the things that junior high and high school students were doing only a few years ago. Yet there is an addiction that makes all others pale in comparison.

We are main-lining an intensely deadlier addiction, called busyness. It is an addiction of epidemic proportions. Church functions, business meetings, soccer games, football practices, dance recitals, movies on multiple channels, sports, MP3 players strapped to our heads and email devices clipped to our belts. The noise of the world is deafening and deadening our spirits and stealing our most precious earthly commodity . . . our hearts.

Over the last 20 years of walking with God we have made an observation: Most of us (Marc and David included) have traded authentic relationship with God and others, for the hustle and bustle of life. We have been anesthetized and inoculated by our culture and surroundings. We have become part of a culture that celebrates the addiction of work-aholism and productivity. We have been numbed to the deepest places of our hearts. Like a steady dose of pain-killer, given enough time it always works. And it has.

We celebrate and encourage it. As crazy as it sounds for us to say that, it is true. The people who have mastered the art of busyness are the ones we want to hire. They are the people who know how to "multi-task." We thrive on it. We admire it in others. We somehow, strangely, need it. It is like a drug.

Many of us have believed the lie that we function better when we are busy. We have embraced a notion that we must fly through our days at a neck-breaking pace. Our fear of falling behind, being left out and feeling inadequate is our fuel for this journey. Strangely enough, what we are burning out is ourselves. We can't sit down. We don't want to sit down. We would like to, but we are afraid that if we do, the world will blow right by and leave us in its wake.

MARC

COMFORTABLE IN CHAOS

Many years ago, I was going through some counseling. The counselor was tenacious in his insistence that I had to slow down, calm my mind. After several weeks of his prodding, I became agitated with the counselor. Not true. He just ticked me off! When he poked me this time, I twisted off. "Sir, this thing you are describing may work for you. I always think so much better when chaos is happening around me. I thrive in the busyness. I am better in the noise. Things are clearer in the noise. In fact, when things get crazy, I am at my best. When it gets quiet . . . now that's when I get nervous. Back off! You don't understand; I work better when it is loud."

No truer word had I ever spoken. Quietness was not my ally, it was my enemy. I did not like quiet. Noise was my drug of choice to hide the pain in my soul and spirit. As long as everyone and everything in my life was in chaos, I was great (at least I thought I was). I unknowingly ran from quietness and solitude.

Quietness forced me to deal with me. Quietness forced me out of the "ministry" and to look at my life, my wounds and my weaknesses. Quietness forced me to look in the mirror and gaze on the reflection of what I had become: a motley bag of emotions, expectations and wounds. Because of this potential run-in with myself I chose to NOT be left alone. I couldn't stand being left alone.

As I look back on my life, I now have an entirely different perspective. I see that I was unaware of the stark difference between external comfort and inward peace.

Marc

External comfort can come in many different packages and forms. The right job, a pill, adequate attention, sexual fantasy and fulfillment, alcohol, validation, titles and success. External comfort is temporary relief in an on-going, internal turmoil. It is the quick fix. It is the instantly-gratifying antidote that eases the pain and relieves the stress. But it is always temporary.

Internal peace, on the other hand, is from God. It is an internal reality of the presence and power of God. Internal peace, an inside-out Peace is available despite external conditions. The power of peace overrides all external conditions. It resides in my insides; in my spirit and in my soul. Internal peace comes from heaven itself. Peace is other-worldly. It's not from around here. It is from God. And it is dispensed in the Sanctuary of your heart. As a matter of fact, peace was designed specifically for the human heart!

Most of us have two primary reasons we don't take God up on the offer to come away with Him. First, we are afraid to allow God to deal with our past and the hurt tucked away in the secret places of our hearts. On a deeper and more frightening level, we are afraid that when we get still, God won't speak to us. Deep in all of us there is an unfounded fear that we won't hear Him when and if He speaks. We have talked to countless people who have said different variations on this theme: "I have tried it, and I have never really heard Him say anything to me."

A TRIP TO THE TREE HOUSE

When was the last time you sat under a tree or in a park and just spent a couple of hours with God? When was the last time that your world intersected with the high, holy one of heaven? When was the last time you really stepped out of your busyness and noise and spent time alone?

"He gives strength to the weary and increases the power of the weak. Even youths grow tired and weary, and young men stumble and fall; but those who hope in the LORD will renew their strength. They will soar on wings like eagles; they will run and not grow weary, they will walk and not be faint."

(Isaiah 40:29-31 NIV)

Are you sick and tired of being sick and tired? Is anyone out there weary? Is anyone out there about to faint? Come on, somebody shout for joy! This is a promise from the heart of God to you. God is inviting us to come away to a secret place and the safety of His presence. In His presence is a promise of renewal. In His presence is the place of restoration. In His presence is the longed-for place of sanctuary. It is the place that you have dreamed about and wished it could be true.

"You have made known to me the path of life; you fill me with joy in your presence, with eternal pleasures at your right hand" *(Psalm 16:11 NIV).* Are you tired of the pace of your life? Are you tired of doing? Would you like to be filled with joy? Would you like "to be" instead of "do"? Are you tired of running? I don't know any runner who can run and not grow weary. Yet God is offering us spirit power beyond our own strengths and abilities. It is beyond your weaknesses and limitations. Real power is found in the secret place. The secret place is truly where heaven invades earth. It is the place of spiritual collision. It is a place where God breathes His breath of life into our tired and worn out souls.

King David said it this way: "O Lord, you have examined my heart and know everything about me. You know when I sit down and when I stand up. You know my thoughts even when I'm far away. You see me when I travel and when I rest at home. You

*know everything I do. You know what I am going to say even
before I say it, Lord. You go before me and follow me. You
place your hand of blessing on my head. Such knowledge is too
wonderful for me, too great for me to understand!" (Psalm 139:
1-6 NLT).*

God longs for His children to walk in the cool of the morning,
the hot of the day or late in the evening with Him. He wants to
walk with us through every season of life. It is only when we
come away with Him that He breathes true life into us. We have
ravenously consumed busyness in exchange for true life . . .
real life.

We have forgotten how to be alone and meditate with and on God.
For most of us, when we hear the word "meditate," we tend to
think about a monk chanting in Latin. It sounds like some strange
mixture of New Age teaching and mystical Christianity. However,
the more we have studied God's Word, we have discovered
that meditation is a biblical term.

Webster's Dictionary defines meditate: to muse over, to
contemplate, ponder, to engage in deep mental exercise directed
towards a heightened level of spiritual awareness.

Contemplate. Ponder. Engage. Do we really have time for that?
Most of us don't act like it. Far too many times we read our daily
devotionals, check it off our "to-do list" and move on with the day.
In the blur of busyness, our devotional life can become something
that we do instead of something that we are. We read God's Word
like we are punching a time clock. We put in our time and then go
on to the next thing. We read, but more often than not, miss the
principles that could possibly change our lives forever. We don't

wait long enough to allow our hearts to become like His. We fail to meditate and ponder on the words that we have read.

THE ONE THING

Okay, this is going to sound very strange coming from two men who just wrote a book. However, we want to make one thing crystal clear: Reading this book will not change your life. I am sure that you wish we had said that a little earlier. But it is true. Information won't change you. Neither will more discipline. Another conference or retreat will not change you. The only force in the universe that can truly change you is the presence and the power of God.

We have been pecking at you now for nine chapters. Do you get it yet? It's about the heart. It's about sanctuary. Have you discovered it? Listen very closely. YOU MUST DO ONE THING. You must get alone with God. You must! You must! You must stop doing Christianity and start being a Christian, a child of God. You must cease your life as a human doing and become a human being. You must stop the noise. You must take the time. You must choose His presence in the tree house.

Are you so busy doing that you have stopped being? Have you traded some One who is Real for some thing that is counterfeit?

> "As Jesus and the disciples continued on their way to Jerusalem, they came to a certain village where a woman named Martha welcomed him into her home. Her sister, Mary, sat at the Lord's feet, listening to what he taught. But Martha was distracted by the big dinner she was preparing. She came to Jesus and said, 'Lord, doesn't it seem unfair to you that my sister just sits here while I do all the work? Tell her to come and help me.'

"But the Lord said to her, 'My dear Martha, you are worried and upset over all these details! There is only one thing worth being concerned about. Mary has discovered it, and it will not be taken away from her.'"

(Luke 10:38-42 NLT)

Mary and Martha welcomed Jesus into their home. Martha chose the big dinner. Mary chose Jesus . . . the one thing. And Jesus said that it (He) could not be taken away from her. Let somebody else do the work for a while. Sit down at His feet. Let Him talk for a while.

What do you need to hear? What do you long to hear? Do you need to hear it from your Heavenly Father? Will you choose the One Thing?

Mary, Martha, Marc, David, Rhonda, Jeff, Paul, Brian, Melissa, Ellie . . . what will you choose? Who will you choose? There is only One. He is the One and Only. He who fashioned your heart and gave you breath and life waits for you. He is the One Thing.

Get out of your routine. Go away with God. Go to a park. Lock yourself in a hotel room. Sit in your backyard. Build a fire in your backyard and sit down. Run! Don't walk. Find a spot. Make the time. Clear your calendar. Kill the noise. Stop the busyness and arrest the traffic in your mind. Get alone. Your Friend is waiting. He wants to speak to you heart to heart.

Come up to the tree house again. And this time . . . bring your stuff.

JOURNAL

JOURNAL

— Chapter 2 —

"I went to the woods because I wished to live deliberately . . .
And not, when I came to die, discover that I had not lived."

HENRY DAVID THOREAU

"The tragedy of life is what dies inside of a man while he lives."

ALBERT SCHWEITZER

"Our deepest fear is not that we are inadequate.
Our deepest fear is that we are powerful beyond measure.
It is our light, not our darkness, that most frightens us.
We ask ourselves, who am I to be brilliant, gorgeous, talented,
and fabulous? Actually, who are you not to be? You are a child
of God. Your playing small doesn't serve the world. There's
nothing enlightened about shrinking so that other people
won't feel insecure around you. We are all meant to shine,
as children do. We are born to make manifest the glory of God
that is within us. It's not just in some of us, it's in everyone.
And as we let our own light shine, we unconsciously give other
people permission to do the same. As we are liberated from our
own fear, our presence automatically liberates others."

FROM THE MOTION PICTURE

AKEELAH AND THE BEE

(2006)

— Chapter 3 —

"Denial is the worst sort of heart disease known to mankind.
In denying the image displayed in the mirror
We unknowingly dismiss freedom and cease to exist."

ANONYMOUS

*"We long to be known and we fear it like nothing else.
Most people live with subtle dread that one day they will be
discovered for who they really are and the world will be appalled."*

SACRED ROMANCE - PAGE 84
THOMAS NELSON - 1997

— Chapter 4 1/2 —

"Everybody is normal until you get to know them."

JOHN ORTBERG

— Chapter 5 —

*"More life may trickle out of a man through thought
than through a gaping wound."*

THOMAS HARDY

— Chapter 6 —

"And about that time God showed up."

FORREST GUMP

— Chapter 6 1/2 —

*"No man for any considerable period, can wear one face
to himself, and another to the multitudes, without finally getting
bewildered as to which may be true."*

NATHANIEL HAWTHORNE

— Chapter 7 —

*"Too many people, too many demands, too much to do, competent,
busy, hurrying people – it just isn't living at all."*

ANN MORROW LINDBERGH

Elevate Ministries is dedicated to motivating and igniting people in a daily walk with Jesus Christ. By communicating biblical principles that foster growth and maturity, we encourage individuals to walk in their God-given destiny and purpose. Whether we are sharing the message of Jesus Christ in a church, business, conference or on the mission field, we desire to promote, encourage and connect people to a passionate life with Jesus Christ!

PROMOTE. ENCOURAGE. CONNECT

7105 GOLF CLUB DRIVE, SUITE 1205

FT WORTH, TX 76179 | 817.236.3436

WWW.ELEVATEHIM.COM